To many Hoosiers, Jerry Pattengale has become the Garrison Keillor of their beloved state. Take, read, smile, laugh and when done, leave Jerry's work on the doorstep of a hardened enemy (if needed, I fear I can loan you one or two).

—**Todd C. Ream**
Distinguished Professor, Taylor University

A great teacher and a great teacher of teachers, Jerry Pattengale is a true believer that teaching and learning can change lives, the lives of both students and teachers. In a world where it is easy to blame teachers, students or colleges for what education does not do, Jerry embraces teachers, students, and even colleges in possibilities. His enthusiasm reminds us all of what teaching and learning can rightly mean in the world.

—**Patrick E. White**
President Emeritus, Wabash College

A pithy and powerful exploration of the notion of objectivity, which will be welcomed by all students of biblical history and interpretation [for *Biblical Evidence*].

—**Alister McGrath**
University of Oxford, Andreas Idreos Professorship in
Science and Religion, Faculty of Theology and Religion

Jerry Pattengale is one of those rare writers who deftly weaves erudite scholarship, wisdom, and homespun humor into compelling and enjoyable reading experiences. He is always a worthwhile intellectual and spiritual companion.

—**David Wright**
President, Indiana Wesleyan University

IS THE BIBLE AT FAULT?

How the Bible Has Been
Misused to Justify Evil,
Suffering, and Bizarre Behavior

JERRY PATTENGALE Ph.D.

WORTHY®
PUBLISHING

Published by Worthy Books, an imprint of Worthy Publishing Group, a division of Worthy Media, Inc., One Franklin Park, 6100 Tower Circle, Suite 210, Franklin, TN 37067.

WORTHY is a registered trademark of Worthy Media, Inc.

HELPING PEOPLE EXPERIENCE THE HEART OF GOD

eBook available wherever digital books are sold.

Library of Congress Cataloging-in-Publication Data

Names: Pattengale, Jerry A., author.
Title: Is the Bible at fault? : how the Bible has been misused to justify
  evil, suffering, and bizarre behavior / Jerry Pattengale.
Description: Franklin, TN : Worthy Publishing, 2018. | Includes
  bibliographical references and index.
Identifiers: LCCN 2018034308 | ISBN 9781945470691 (trade paper : alk. paper)
Subjects: LCSH: Bible--Controversial literature. | Bible--Hermeneutics.
Classification: LCC BS533 .P38 2018 | DDC 220.1--dc23
LC record available at https://lccn.loc.gov/2018034308

Unless otherwise noted, Scripture quotations are taken from the ESV Bible (The Holy Bible, English Standard Version®), copyright © 2001 by Crossway, a publishing ministry of Good News Publishers. Used by permission. All rights reserved. | Scripture quotations marked NIV are taken from the Holy Bible, New International Version®, NIV®. Copyright © 1973, 1978, 1984, 2011 by Biblica, Inc.™ Used by permission of Zondervan. All rights reserved worldwide. www.zondervan.com. The "NIV" and "New International Version" are trademarks registered in the United States Patent and Trademark Office by Biblica, Inc.™ | Scripture quotations marked KJV are taken from the Holy Bible, King James Version.

For foreign and subsidiary rights, contact rights@worthypublishing.com

Cover Images: GJFFWM, Nick Young / Alamy Stock Photo; JEJNKF, Robert Clay / Alamy Stock Photo; KFB43M, MMphotos / Alamy Stock Photo; G1DJTH, World History Archive / Alamy Stock Photo; Kt5C6X, Archive PL / Alamy Stock Photo; F0K6MJ, ABC Collection / Alamy Stock Photo; EG6T2F, Everett Collection Historical / Alamy Stock Photo; 638465842, Jorisvo / iStock by Getty Images

Interior Images: F0K6MJ, ABC Collection / Alamy Stock Photo; Shiloh Mansion, Jerry Pattengale; D88AWP, Chronicle / Alamy Stock Photo; G1DKJF, World History Archive / Alamy Stock Photo; G6T2F, Everett Collection Historical / Alamy Stock Photo; KT5C6X, Archive PL / Alamy Stock Photo; 1012578028, The LIFE Picture Collection / Getty Images; E997T0, AF Fotografie / Alamy Stock Photo; DWMMH9, PRISMA ARCHIVO / Alamy Stock Photo; GE72WX, AF Fotografie / Alamy Stock Photo; P1H1H9, World Archive / Alamy Stock Photo; KWD8PB, Everett Collection Inc / Alamy Stock Photo; Illustration by Branford Clarke, Heroes of the Fiery Cross (1928); KT3MBX, Archive PL / Alamy Stock Photo; DC9HCN, North Wind Picture Archives / Alamy Stock Photo; M14AYN, Classic Image / Alamy Stock Photo; KFB43M, MMphotos / Alamy Stock Photo; G1DJTH, World History Archive / Alamy Stock Photo

Author Photo: Courtesy of Jer Nelsen

Cover Design: Charles Brock, Spencer Fuller, Faceout Studio
Interior Design and Typesetting: Bart Dawson

ISBN: 978-1-94547-069-1

Printed in the United States of America
18 19 20 21 22 LBM 8 7 6 5 4 3 2 1

To Dr. Charles Buregeya Mugisha ("Pastor Charles")
and his wife, Florence, for using the Bible
to facilitate positive transformation in Rwanda

CONTENTS

INTRODUCTION

"All things are lawful," but not all things are helpful.
"All things are lawful," but not all things build up.
Let no one seek his own good, but the good of his neighbor.

1 CORINTHIANS 10:23–24

S ome people do weird things. Other people are just plain strange—perpetually odd. Unfortunately, some people are sinister, and a few are all the above. From the curious to the criminal, whether acting in isolation or as instigators of revolutions and institutions, many have claimed biblical authority for their actions. They have hitched their ideological wagons to inept interpretations of biblical statements. Throughout history, this hodgepodge of public figures has prompted people to ask, *Is the Bible at fault?*

Little has changed since the earliest known stories from the ancient Near East, including stories of wayward characters in the Bible. People have made bizarre or dangerous claims in the name of God. They continue to do so, often citing biblical passages—out of context or inappropriately—as proof texts. The severity of their missteps has led to a wide range of disasters, from selling child pilgrims during the Crusades, to executing other Christians for theological differences, to wild activities in the name of evangelism.

As we process some of these weird, strange, odd, and even sinister stories, ultimately, there are two aspects of the same project: (1) identifying teachings that create unnecessary victims where misinterpretations have led to people being abused or misused in the name of the Bible, and (2) promoting a responsible and Christ-centered interpretation wherever possible. If we get the Bible right, we will naturally eliminate victims and allow Christ in the Bible to be the Word of God and a force of good in every text and context.

This agenda is not always as easy as it sounds. The Bible contains some difficult texts; it's easy to misread or, worse, to abuse it and make it a tool for cruelty or manipulation. Let's face it: some people are strange. Spend five minutes watching people's antics on YouTube or scrolling through sites like PeopleofWalmart.com and you'll see a stream of warped behavior across the social spectrum. It's not limited to those espousing biblical authority.

The human condition is one filled with knowledge of good and evil (consider the tree in Eden) and all the fruit that comes with knowing both. Human tendencies remain the same since the time of Abraham and the Patriarchs, with the capacity for both noble and ignoble motives, marvels and miseries, caring and corruption, and creative expression. This side of the Garden of Eden, we are all fallen creatures. This side of Easter, we all have hope for redemptive outcomes— as individuals and as a community.

Throughout the world, we can visit cities with reminders of both brilliant leaders of biblical interpretation and noted detractors. In the pages that follow, we will visit many of the latter, such as Jan of Leiden, whose heretical teachings led to the 1535 massacre in Münster, Germany. Contemporary with his misdeeds was the work of the great biblical scholar, Erasmus, whose printed Greek New Testament helped enhance biblical studies (and influenced the Protestant Reformation).

On one side of the ledger is an infamous heretic and on the other a language scholar helping generations to have a clearer understanding of the New Testament in its original language.

So, let us ask the question to Jan of Leiden and Erasmus: *Is the Bible at fault for their legacies, the outcomes of their lives?* For Erasmus, the answer is Yes. The Bible was the fulcrum of his life, and he worked feverishly to maintain its integrity. The Bible was behind everything he did and certainly "at fault" for what his life became and the projects he undertook. He brought back one of the Bible's original languages to check the later Latin version popularized by St. Jerome. Roman Catholic scholars and those who would become "reformers" used Erasmus's text. Both interpreters, Jan of Leiden and Erasmus, started with the Bible but ended up in rather different places.

For Jan of Leiden and heretics of his ilk, the Bible certainly is not at fault for their heresies. Jan of Leiden, like most heretics, amended its teachings, added radical and untenable interpretations, and used the texts for his own advantage. For some heretics like Jan, the latter seems paramount. For others, their heresies don't appear as self-promotion but merely misplaced passion and beliefs. The Bible's core teachings are not open to rewritten meanings and manifestos that give permission for what the same Bible clearly declares as sin.

In the chapters ahead, we will look at several stories that have prompted onlookers, whether contemporaries or students of history, to question the Bible's value. Each time we will show how those involved followed a path similar to Leiden. In most of these stories, we can look at a few key leaders that led others, sometimes millions of victims, astray.

These stories continue to surface in an increasingly global and crowded world. Sometimes, we find various responses to biblical themes and commands within close proximity to one another. To illustrate this, consider one afternoon in Rome that I experienced only a few years ago. I saw radically different religious choices play out with three people a few hundred yards apart near St. Peter's Basilica.

During breakfast in the Casa Santa Marta, the Vatican's lodging for visiting cardinals and invited guests, a friend pointed out Cardinal Bergoglio from Argentina and whispered, "He's likely the next pope." The smiling priest was there, cloaked in tradition and collecting leftover milk from others' tables, most likely to keep it from going to waste. His concern for resources flows from his understanding of biblical texts. He has since become the 266th pope, Pope Francis—the most recognizable face of institutional Christianity.

A few minutes later, while walking through the elliptical array of columns in the Braccio di Carlo Magno (the Charlemagne Wing, or "arm"), I saw the most bizarre thing, something rather unexpected—a skull face. As I passed by the last of the stately columns, a fellow was finishing a conversation and suddenly turned around. We almost danced as we tried to move past each other. With our faces only a few feet apart, I froze momentarily and tried not to flinch or gawk while maintaining eye contact. He had tattooed his entire face and bald head to look like a creepy, skinless skull with sunken eyes. From the lips down, he sported a tattooed cobweb—a permanent beard. His lips had painted stitches that appeared to hold them shut. His forehead had bone cracks, and his eyes were ensconced in black pools. Then it struck me that, given his visit to the Vatican, he was likely a worshiper of *Nuestra Señora de la Santa Muerte*, which translates in English, "Our Lady of Holy Death." His ink-laden actions likely flowed from his understanding of biblical references to death, despite the Catholic Church's uncompromising condemnation of all worship of this personification of death, which has a strong following among

Catholics with Mexican heritage (different from but related to Walt Disney's blockbuster 2017 film, *Coco*, which celebrates ancestors' spiritual journey around "The Day of the Dead" holiday). This individual had found this personification of death to be compatible with worship of Jesus Christ, who Scripture describes as "the life" (John 11:25). Somehow, he thought it was possible to worship death *and also* not believe that, "The last enemy to be destroyed is death" (1 Corinthians 15:26).

Within a few more steps, I ran across the third person in this episode. In the pedestrian underpass on Via Delle Fornaci, an elderly religious sister was begging alms for the poor. For weeks afterward, I found her there dressed in her worn cloak and laying in a prostrate position—kissing the sidewalk all day, every day. I usually put a euro in her cup, believing I was aiding the poor. I later got a rude awakening when I recognized her in a video sting operation that aired shortly thereafter in the media. According to the report, a woman in her midtwenties was posing as an older nun, and I realized this was the "elderly" woman I had seen. The religious devotion that attracted me and other donors was really a sinister ploy.[1]

Within a few hundred yards, next to one of the holiest sites in Christendom, I had witnessed firsthand three types of expressions associated with biblical teachings. A future pope was cloaked in tradition and dogma. A man worshiped death itself. A greedy con woman posed as a sister of the poor. And, as a tourist, I even participated by watching, discussing, and giving money to these demonstrations. Each action flowed from an understanding of biblical teachings.

We have unlimited possibilities on how to behave here on earth and how to prepare for the hereafter. Either by design or default, we all make such choices every day. History also testifies that each generation has its share of weird, strange, and sinister events—often in the name of religion, and all too often driven by skewed biblical interpretations.

If you have a vibrant faith in the historic death and resurrection of Jesus Christ, you may look at these events through a different lens than much of the world. Perhaps the most famous quotation of Karl Marx, long associated with the ills of Communism, is his 1843 phrase, "It [religion] is the opium of the people" (commonly quoted as "Religion is the opiate of the masses"). That is to say, according to Marx, religion is like a drug. It is a self-induced (or concocted) aid to get through crises and pain or to find comfort in spiritual illusions. It is practical. Perhaps some of the sinister uses and perversions of Christianity had such sway—but this is not representative of the historical realities of Christ or his teachings.

It is indeed difficult to pinpoint the motives of the many misuses of the Bible for unfortunate ends. However, it is sensible to assume that many religious expressions outside of orthodox biblical truths have attracted masses because of the leaders' illusionary power over followers. Too often, the leaders have wielded totalitarian control with selfish communal, national, or global ramifications.

That level of control over large groups of people has led many into the realm of the bizarre. That's right, *bizarre*. As we explore twelve different cases of abhorrent behavior in the name of Scripture, we can't be afraid to call these things what they are. These have been terrible, destructive movements that have led people astray, brought irreparable spiritual and emotional harm, and even cost countless people their lives. The members of the Ku Klux Klan, for example, had no doubt that their actions were justified in the eyes of God. The murderous armies of the Fourth Crusade were grateful for the chance to slay other

Christians in the name of the church. Tanchelm of Antwerp brought his congregation to their feet with cheers celebrating his marriage to an inanimate statue of the Virgin Mary. Detroit's Prophet Jones locked his followers in all-night revival meetings and often wouldn't let them out until they made financial contributions to the cause—the *cause* being his lavish lifestyle of fancy cars, hundreds of suits, and fur coats. Christian missionaries not only condoned the wholesale slaughter of Australia's native Aborigine people, they *participated* in it—with clean consciences, no less. These are real, historical people and events, and we'll explore every one of them and more in these pages.

We'll walk through each case study like your favorite crime-scene investigator on television, first trying to understand what happened and then breaking down the biblical errors and abuses that led to these historical disasters. We'll ask, *Is the Bible at fault?* and honestly evaluate whether or not the Bible played the right part in each case. I'll show where and how each teacher and group departed from biblical orthodoxy, identify the types of interpretive problems that are present, and suggest an antidote for preventing such abuses in the future. The goal isn't to bang a gavel and proclaim over and over again, "No, the Bible isn't at fault!" Rather, each chapter is about getting out of the Bible's way so it can reach the hearts of people without distortion. Each chapter has a different lesson for us, but each of these lessons is ultimately about how to avoid harming people with a book that represents their greatest good.[2]

I should point out here at the outset, though, that the Bible is not always an obvious or easy text to interpret. In every case, it requires the mind of Christ and the guidance of the Holy Spirit to truly see what the Word says. It is a living document, and we must approach every biblical encounter with a prayer for wisdom and discernment.

But, apart from the question of inspired reading, many people in history have failed the Bible on a more fundamental level. They read the Bible wrongly, sometimes deliberately and other times because they didn't know how to get it right. This book will be concerned with these kinds of textual problems, misuses, and abuses that are avoidable by reading the Bible responsibly as an ancient text.[3]

As you read through these stories of bizarre behavior, which often put suffering and evil on grotesque display, you will find an obvious omission. I've chosen not to highlight any living leaders or current groups—either fledgling or long-established—that you may know today. The cases you may be most familiar with, snake handling and the Ku Klux Klan, are the closest things to current events you'll find in the book. You can always find a long list of current shady religious dealings, cultic behaviors, and political unrest in the media, but I wanted to avoid those passing headlines here.[4] Instead, I hope this selection of stories provides a wider and more engaging breadth of cases that not only helps diagnose past misuses and abuses, but also provides some helpful frameworks and principles for approaching more recent misuses and abuses.

Jerry Pattengale
July 17, 2018

CHAPTER 1

Sex Scandal of the House of David
in Benton Harbor, Michigan:

Why Veering from Biblical Canon Can Be Explosive

Truly, truly, I say to you, if anyone keeps my word,
he will never see death.

JOHN 8:51

When the Lamb opened the seventh seal, there was silence
in heaven for about half an hour. Then I saw the seven angels
who stand before God, and seven trumpets were given to them.
And another angel came and stood at the altar with a golden
censer, and he was given much incense to offer with the prayers
of all the saints on the golden altar before the throne,
and the smoke of the incense, with the prayers of the saints,
rose before God from the hand of the angel.
Then the angel took the censer and filled it with fire
from the altar and threw it on the earth,
and there were peals of thunder, rumblings,
flashes of lightning, and an earthquake.

REVELATION 8:1–5

Imagine parks crowded with people gazing at eleven Jesus look-alikes playing baseball. For millions of fans, that was their introduction to the Israelite House of David—a cult from Benton Harbor, Michigan, that thrived during the early 1900s. These boys of summer heard the crowds roar as their long flowing hair went airborne while they ran the bases during exhibition games with professional teams. Their pregame "pepper" routines—rapid-fire and lighthearted throwing and fielding exchanges—became their hallmark.

Before we get too caught up on how they entertained the masses, which has been well-documented in many books and newspapers, I should point out that this was indeed a religious cult—and it was destined for a sordid ending.

However, for the crowds, these gifted players in pinstripes looked like Jesus in jammies. The players thought everyone should look like the first-century Nazarene if, that is, they followed the Levitical code of the Old Testament. They also abstained from meat, alcohol, money, profanity, and sex. For such an ascetic group, these men sure exuded a love of life, and they seemed to enjoy all people. Until their leader's scandal rocked their world, they were beloved by all who enjoyed their antics. Besides assisting with numerous community events and functions, they would play a couple hundred games a year!

For them, sports had a unique purpose. Baseball was a communal activity back in their Benton Harbor compound that helped them release some of their pent-up energy as teenagers. It seemed to work, too; by the time they grew to maturity and played big league teams in exhibition settings, they were good enough to win two-thirds of their games!

They became a welcome attraction, especially at Negro League games. Their House of David team hosted years of games against other teams that were likewise marginalized. The Negro League included legendary players such as Satchel Paige and Ernie Banks (before they were allowed in the big national leagues). Some members played more than a hundred games against Satchel, who referred to them affectionately as "the Jesus boys." The Israelite House of David even created basketball teams and toured with the Harlem Globetrotters.

People enjoyed the "Israelites," as they preferred to be called. They were a hoot. They weren't anti-authoritarian or carefree hippies but nice, fun, long-haired members of society. Sure, they had unique religious beliefs, but they were active community members. Members of the Israelite House of David seemed to have the gift of entertainment and were welcomed by their Michigan community and a half-million tourists annually. They thought those who followed true beliefs (theirs) would live forever, so why not have some fun while awaiting Christ's return? Chris Siriano, owner of the House of David Museum in nearby St. Joseph, Michigan, said, "They wanted to have fun; they wanted to invite America into their lives; they loved to entertain and laugh and have a blast. They always told me it was a means to an end, to get them to tomorrow, 'cause tomorrow was when paradise was coming.'"[1]

While the Jehovah's Witnesses believed that Christ would return to their group first at their New York City Watchtower, the Benton Harbor cult waited expectantly for Christ to return first to them in Michigan. They believed the world would receive its just destruction in time, and twelve thousand members from the twelve tribes of Israel—the select of Jesus Christ—would gather in Michigan to usher in a millennium of peace.

While they were awaiting their prophesied millennium, their amusement park, zoo, world's smallest passenger steam engine (nicknamed "Hiawatha"), bowling alley, theater, music stage, traveling bands, and one of the nation's largest farmer's markets drew multitudes of fans. Their impressive Victorian mansions set a pleasant backdrop to all of this grandeur.

This was the curious but fun Israelite House of David. Well, at least to those outsiders intrigued by their actions and aptly named buildings on East Britain Avenue: "Bethlehem," "Jerusalem," and "Shiloh," with their "Diamond House" as the centerpiece made of sparkling concrete. But their headquarters quickly lost its luster after the world awoke to media releases about a late-night raid. The compound's shuttered homes were hiding a monster—the messianic pretender and founder, Benjamin Purnell, who could have doubled for Colonel Custer.

Benjamin "Brother Ben" Purnell was somewhat of a wanderer from a family of twelve in Kentucky and, for a short time, a broom maker in Richmond, Indiana. More importantly, he was a silver-tongued preacher. He and his second wife, Mary, attracted around a thousand followers to the colony they built around his messianic message and stringent taboos. Their followers saw them, especially Brother Ben, as the Seventh Messenger foretold by the apostle John in Revelation 10:1-7. Detractors called him "King Ben," a title members rejected as a sensationalized effort to discredit him. The Seventh Messenger was the final one ushering in the millennium, and he and Mary taught the Benton Harbor Israelites that John 8:51 promised physical immortality to anyone who "keeps [his] word." In other words, he said his group of Israelites would never die. Those who *did* die, therefore, were not true believers, as death became the evidence of a lack of faith. Consequently, members were buried without a ceremony or grave markers somewhere on the colony's properties. Physical death was viewed not as a tragic inevitability, but as a spiritual failure.

This harsh view of the dead was nothing new to the Purnells. Before colonizing Benton Harbor, Benjamin and Mary were run out of town by residents of a small community in Ohio after these nascent prophets refused to identify or bury their daughter when she died in an explosion at the factory where she worked. They were alleged to have responded to the tragedy by quoting Jesus's command to "Let the dead bury their dead" (Luke 9:60 KJV).

What happened in Benton Harbor stayed in Benton Harbor—well, at least until "the axe-wielding State Troopers, accompanied by camera-toting reporters, broke into [Benjamin's] home shortly after midnight on November 17, 1926, and placed him under arrest."[2] The whole ordeal became a national story with all the trappings of intrigue, as David and his wife faced a litany of charges.

Anticipating the raid, the mysterious and magnetic cult founder had whisked away a group of adolescent girls to High Island, the House of David's own remote island in northern Lake Michigan. Thirteen girls would eventually come forward with claims of sexual exploitation. One witness, Isabella Pritchard, claimed the actual number of sexually exploited women among the Israelites was around five hundred. The trial would involve more than a hundred witnesses and more than three hundred pages of court documents, but supporting testimony to Pritchard's claims was lacking, and many testified to Purnell's character.[3] As the world learned about the unique beliefs of the colony, the luster left more than the Diamond House.

The #MeToo campaign wasn't around to save the female virgins from Purnell's spiritual initiation rites. As the curator of a Benton Harbor museum reflects, the Seventh Messenger was determined "to plant the eternal seed within them."[4] Though Judge Louis H. Fead found him and Mary guilty of religious fraud and ordered their exile from the colony, he writes in his official opinion, "His people reverence him. Their love and loyalty are patent. While a despot, he must have been a kindly monarch."[5]

The trial didn't end the House of David story, only Benjamin's reputation. In 1930, Mary separated from the Israelite House of David over a dispute of succession. With her $60,000 settlement, she bought property across the street and began an offshoot group, the City of David. It prospered for another two decades. Even though Judge Fead had ordered the Purnells not to evangelize, new initiates continued to arrive, including a stream of Jews during times of anti-Semitism— so many, in fact, that Mary built a synagogue.

Both colonies thrived and sparked diverse industries. Traditional businesses like lumber and fishing were a mainstay, and more advanced initiatives like bottled water and advanced cold storage quickly sprung up. Some of their inventions allegedly included the rack that arranges bowling pins, the waffle cone, a cross-propeller system for steamships, canning ability for grape juice, and wooden pallets for forklifts. They also developed a special gold painting style out of fish scales, which is on display in Benton Harbor. Between these business endeavors and communal requirements (all initiates handed over all possessions to the group upon joining), the community is believed to have amassed enormous wealth. It's suggested that the current assets of the Israelite House of David exceeds $217 million.[6] A major renovation has taken place on the original campus, now a gated entry, and the facilities are stunning (though the second campus of Mary's City of David is in ill repair, identified clearly with a new Michigan Historic Site sign).[7]

The irony of the entire story, of course, is that both the Purnells died—ah, but with a twist. We will never know exactly what would have transpired if the trial had continued through the system, as Benjamin died a few months after the initial trial ended, which the

Michigan Supreme Court eventually overturned. What he began with such fanfare in 1903 was spiraling downward when he died of tuberculosis in 1927. Benjamin's body is said to be preserved in an upstairs bedroom of the Diamond House so he can rise up and reunite the twelve lost tribes of Israel for the *"Ingathering,"* the gathering of the faithful to await the restoration of Eden on earth (hence the name Eden Springs Park the colony ran for tourists). Likewise, Mary's followers allegedly buried her vertically, anticipating a short stay for her beneath the surface. Her well-appointed tomb, appearing as a vertical mausoleum, is easily visible outside the main occupied residence on the City of David campus. Allegedly, her vertical burial would allow her to exit more quickly at Christ's return.

Today, there are occasional ghost hunts on part of their property, which is now owned by a developer. There is also a room in the Benton Harbor Public Library dedicated to this group, as well as a relatively new House of David Museum in nearby St. Joseph, Michigan. Otherwise, there's little left of Purnell's Israelite House of David community that once wowed so many crowds of cheering baseball fans.

IS THE BIBLE AT FAULT?

The Biblical Outcome

The Israelite House of David wasn't merely another case of a magnetic religious figure having a sex scandal. Along with the City of David, as the two were inextricably linked, the colonies were incredibly resourceful and inventive Christian sects with outsized cultural footprints. In short, their fame and failure revolved around the moral and administrative failures of a leader empowered by a distorted view of biblical prophecy. The heretical theological beliefs and personal actions of its founder hijacked many otherwise admirable kingdom values of this colorful and entrepreneurial community.

The influence of the Bible was evident throughout this group, but that influence was filtered through Brother Ben's unique interpretation. We can get a feel for this in Benjamin's own words, from a publication titled *Benjamin's Last Writing*, written shortly before his death. In the comment below, he explains why the male members of the Israelite House of David were instructed to wear their hair long:

> Why do the Israelites wear long hair and beards? . . . We wear
> long hair because Jesus, who is the pattern and waymark of an
> Israelite, wears it. No matter what nationality makes pictures
> of Christ, they always make Him with long hair, and a beard.
> If God wanted man to have short hair, He would have made
> him with short hair. He should be left as he was made.[8]

The *biblical* reason for this convention wasn't actually biblical at all. In this case, the House of David scriptural canon extended to trends in paintings and Sunday school artwork that are not rooted in

17

the biblical text. The person who Benjamin is referencing and imitating is not the Jesus of the Bible but the Jesus of popular culture.

Another telling example is Benjamin's explanation for why Israelite members of the House of David believed they would never die, taken from this same publication:

> We Israelites of the House of David believe we will never die, while all unbelievers will perish. The body of Jesus, the First-born of Israel, saw not corruption, and that is why we true Israelites live the lives of celibates, eschewing all carnal intercourse, even between man and wife. Sin is a transgression of the Law, and the sting of death is sin, (1 Corinthians 15:56) who reap the wages of sin, which is death (Romans 6:23). Then how could a man who is righteous reap the wages of sin? In the case of righteousness he could not die. So it is written: In the way of righteousness is life, and in the pathway thereof there is no death (Proverbs 12:28).[9]

In this case, he is sticking with the Bible but only with narrow and selective readings—and gaps in logic doom his interpretation. We'll talk more about this second example in the next section.

Point of Departure from Biblical Orthodoxy

In some ways, the House of David is a prime example of how one's misuse of the Bible can lead to abuse. A huge misstep was their acceptance of nonbiblical writings, such as the prophecies of the nineteenth-century evangelist John Wroe, as authoritative scripture. Then, if that wasn't bad enough, they misread, misinterpreted, and misapplied the actual text of the New Testament itself. These errors resulted in flaws that doomed a community with a lot of admirable qualities.

We'll look at some of these issues of deviation and interpretation in closer detail. But for the moment, we might just acknowledge them and hear from a former House of David member, H. M. Williams. He refers to Purnell's relationship to the Bible in the following critiques written shortly after Williams left the group in 1907. These comments come from a small publication titled *Mysteries, Errors and Injustice at Mary and Benjamin's Israelite House of David*. On Brother Ben's approach to reading the Bible, Williams writes:

> Benjamin continues to fix the scriptures to suit himself, leaving out phrases or words or changing them entirely, substituting words where he wants them, changing the word "and" for "but," taking out the word "not" where it is objectionable to his theory. This is the way that he got on with his interpretations.[10]

In another passage, Williams destroys Purnell's claim that believers will never die. How so? By quoting passage after passage from the Bible that clearly speak to the death that comes to all men, faithful or not. Such passages include Hebrews 9:27, Psalm 82:7, 1 Corinthians 15:36, and many more.

On Purnell's presentation of himself as the second coming of Jesus Christ, Williams asserts he could "profit . . . to know there is but one God and one mediator between God and man, the man Christ Jesus, 1 Timothy 2:5."[11] On his behavior with women, Williams dismisses Purnell's claims that such interactions were merely innocent interactions by claiming Purnell had a specific type of woman—which he described as always "young," "plump," and "fair"—who claimed all his attention and "fondling."[12] According to this firsthand account of life within the walls of the Israelite House of David, there can be little

19

question that the founder was guilty of the crimes for which he was accused.

Problem Type

These are just a few of the issues and conflicts we encounter when we lose accountability to the Bible. This also shows the result of separating ourselves from the accountability of church leadership that the biblical text encourages. Furthermore, it's a prime example of what can happen when we try to improve on the Bible or grant our faith leaders more authority than we ascribe to the Bible. Close-knit communities and strong leaders are important, but they can never be set above the Word of God. And, of course, this case study shows us plenty of bad exegesis too.

ANTIDOTE

We have to allow the Bible to be itself. We need to honor its breadth and limitations. We should focus on its message, rather than on its commentators, and study and interpret it responsibly. A great deal of resources are available to help you study the Bible. Consider checking out the resources on the Evangelical Christian Publishers Association site. If you are from an orthodox Christian community outside the evangelical faith tradition, consult your denomination's or religious branch's publishing house.

One of the more humorous (and sad) assessments of the House of David's struggles comes from former member Bert Johnson, who thought highly of the group's often biblical community values. "Best religion I know of," he says. "Only problem was, Benjamin wasn't living it."[13] We might apply Johnson's comment to Benjamin's relationship to the Bible itself.

Let the story of Brother Ben and the Israelite House of David serve as a cautionary tale as we work through some other bizarre and sometimes sinister misuses of the Bible. It is the Word of God and the best book we know. The only problem with it is the fact that so many so-called Christians aren't living it.

You shall not add to the word that I command you,
nor take from it, that you may keep the commandments
of the LORD your God that I command you.
DEUTERONOMY 4:2

I warn everyone who hears the words of the prophecy of this book:
if anyone adds to them, God will add to him the plagues
described in this book, and if anyone takes away from
the words of the book of this prophecy, God will take away
his share in the tree of life and in the holy city,
which are described in this book.
REVELATION 22:18–19

CHAPTER 2

Vulgarizing the Sacraments:

Take This Cup . . . of Human Blood

Whoever, therefore, eats the bread or drinks
the cup of the Lord in an unworthy manner
will be guilty concerning
the body and blood of the Lord.

1 CORINTHIANS 11:27

Many of the Romans believed that the followers of Jesus the Nazarene, the *Christus*, were deranged. They already viewed this upstart group of his adherents as atheists—for not following the Roman Imperial cult. Most of these Christians refused to show minimal allegiance via a token incense offering to the emperor (the self-proclaimed, deified ruler). In the Romans' minds, these Christ-followers were worse than other atheists because they allegedly participated in horrifying and degrading activities. Romans spread stories about Christians eating aborted babies for religious meals and using semen and menstrual blood for "holy" communion. The stories that Roman citizens shared about Christians likely shocked even the most raucous among the crowds.

The sad part of this scenario is that some of these stories were true. Like exotic ritualistic scenes from the controversial modern thriller *The Da Vinci Code,* an overemphasized offshoot of the early church espoused radical and esoteric practices.

According to early sources, the Phibionites were a small Gnostic sect. Gnosticism, though somewhat complex and with various strands, was classified by Christians as a heresy. Prominent church leaders like Irenaeus firmly rejected Gnostic views of a secret or special knowledge that enabled Gnostics to perceive themselves as the spiritual elite. Gnostics also had a disdain for the material world, an emphasis on the spiritual world, and Docetic views that Christ only *appeared* to die on the cross.[1]

Although some Gnostic sects were ascetic and against sex, others, such as the Phibionites, were much less concerned with propriety. Before we look any further into their bizarre practices, we must recognize (as the early church leaders did) that the "biblical" text the Gnostics followed was considered a corrupted text. This corruption caused them to add a litany of other sacred texts to their teachings.

They were certainly vocal about their views. Both Christians and pagans reviled Gnostics for their beliefs and some sects for their vile ceremonies and routines.

The Phibionites may have stemmed from the Nicolaites, a Gnostic group condemned in Revelation 2 and tied through other writers to similar beliefs. In Revelation, the apostle John relays Christ's words to the Ephesians, praising them for not tolerating "those who are evil," and finding them "to be false" (Revelation 2:2). Citing the words of Jesus, he states, "You hate the works of the Nicolaitans, which I also hate" (Revelation 2:6). Later in this same passage, Jesus warns the church of Pergamum for not rejecting the Nicolaitans (Revelation 2:15).

If Bishop Isidore of Seville (d. AD 636) is correct, part of this ongoing heresy began with its founder, Nicolaus, a deacon ordained by St. Peter for the church of Jerusalem. Nicolaus, says Isidore, "abandoned his wife because of her beauty, so that whoever wanted to might enjoy her; the practice turned into debauchery, with partners being exchanged in turn."[2] As we find in extended passages below from a much earlier writer, Epiphanius of Salamis (late fourth century), this type of activity was rampant among the Phibionites. He too blasts Nicolaus: "In turn these Gnostics have sprouted up in the world, deluded people who have grown from Nicolaus like fruit from a dunghill. . . . These despicable, erring founders of the sects come at us [orthodox Christians] and assault us like a swarm of insects, infecting us with diseases, smelly eruptions, and sores through their error with its mythology."[3]

The Phibionites were a tiny sect, seemingly insignificant by their size alone. However, the stories of their deeds spread throughout the Roman world and sadly influenced many Romans' ideas of what *Christians* really were—despite the fact that Christians deemed them to be heretics. Robert Wilken prompts us to keep the Roman perspective in mind if we are to understand the Roman disdain for early Christians. His book's title summarizes his emphasis: *The Christians as the Romans Saw Them.* This backdrop—where Romans issued charges against these *atheists*—helps us understand why Emperor Nero (d. AD 68) could find a welcome audience in falsely accusing Christians of burning part of Rome (which he himself may have started, as it helped him clear a place for his Golden Palace). This perception of Christians might also be why he could burn Christians as torches in his gardens and why crowds would chant for their public executions in the arenas. These blanket charges were made against all Christians, even though most Christians would be disgusted by the Phibionites' practices. In fact, writers like Justin Martyr worked hard to encourage Romans not to convict someone simply for claiming to be a Christian. The generalizations also led many Christians to speak against heretical sects for fear of being associated with them.

So, what were these horrible practices? Let us take a closer look at the bizarre and sordid world of the Phibionites, who were also called Barbalites, Borborites, Koddians, Secundians, and Socratites, among other names. Perhaps the label *Borborite* captures best their practices. From the Greek word for mud, *borboros,* an easy case can be made that the Romans adapted this foreign word and derogatorily called them the *filthy people.*

Epiphanius's magnum opus, the *Panarion*, gives some of the sinister, bawdy, dehumanizing details of this group. His work's title literally means *medicine chest*, and it contains antidotes for some sixty Christian heresies. An alternate title often used is *Against Heresies.* After it covers a litany of "pre-Christian" heresies, the book contains a stream of analogies of more than fifty animals (heretics and heresies) preying on the true (orthodox) Christians—much like the Nicolaitans mentioned in Revelation preyed on the churches at Ephesus and Pergamum.

Epiphanius wrote his text between AD 374 and 377—only 260 years or so after the Gospel of John was written—yet he could already list sixty Christian heresies. He wrote nearly halfway between two key events that defined Christian orthodoxy. On one end was the Council of Nicaea convened by Emperor Constantine in AD 325, which resulted in the Nicene Creed. On the other end, about fifty years after the *Panarion,* St. Augustine wrote his twenty-two-book tome, *The City of God.* Epiphanius and Augustine are but two of a list of early church leaders who wrote against heresies, mentioning the actions of the Phibionites in their writings.[4]

The Phibionites surfaced as one of the most bizarre and despised of the wide spectrum of Gnostics and were even criticized by other Gnostics.[5] Epiphanius claimed that his reports were instrumental in having members of this group expelled from Alexandria. Even today, his words are perhaps the best insight into their sordid ways. In his *Panarion,* he dissects the Phibionites' various religious statements, ludicrous religious doctrines, and gross misrepresentations of Old and New Testament passages. He also gives rather explicit examples of their sinful practices and reveals that, in his youth, he had come across a group of about eighty in Egypt. Although tempted to join them, he sensed that it was Satan's doing and reported the group to the bishop. They were all removed from the town. In a long diatribe against this heresy, Epiphanius writes:

> Now in telling these stories and others like them, those who have yoked themselves to Nicolaus' sect for the sake of "knowledge" have lost the truth and not merely perverted their

converts' minds, but have also enslaved their bodies and souls to fornication and promiscuity. They foul their supposed assembly itself with the dirt of promiscuous fornication and eat and handle both human flesh and uncleanness. . . . they hold their wives in common. And if a guest who is of their persuasion arrives, they have a sign that men give women and women give men, a tickling of the palm as they clasp hands in supposed greeting, to show that the visitor is of their religion.[6]

After various details about the gatherings and numerous apologies for what readers are about to read, he then describes husbands turning over their wives to "perform the Agape with the brother," or, their version of spiritual sexual intercourse.[7] This gave a new meaning to "brotherly love" in their eyes. Here is an excerpt of his account:

For after having made love with the passion of fornication in addition, to lift their blasphemy up to heaven, the woman and man receive the man's emission on their own hands. And they stand with their eyes raised heavenward put the filth on their hands and pray, if you please—the ones they call Stratiotics and Gnostics—and offer that stuff on their hands to the true Father of all, and say, "We offer thee this gift, the body of Christ." And then they eat it partaking of their own dirt, and say, "This is the body of Christ; and this is the Pascha, because of which our bodies suffer and are compelled to acknowledge the passion of Christ."[8]

As if this isn't enough, the account speaks also about the blood of Christ:

And so with the woman's emission when she happens to be having her period—they likewise take the unclean menstrual blood they gather from her, and eat it in common. And "This," they say, "is the blood of Christ." And so, when they read, "I saw a tree bearing twelve manner of fruits every year, and he said unto me, "This is the tree of life," in apocryphal writings, they interpret this allegorically of the menstrual flux.[9]

So, it's little wonder this small group was able to bring such tarnish to the name *Christian* throughout the Roman world!

Philosophically, the Phibionites strove in everything they did to promote unity. The unity of God was the primordial existence to which all of creation needed to return. Rather than be unified, they claimed, humans used their procreative powers to create disunity. Christ, on the other hand, worked to unify all flesh, and the Phibionites endeavored to do the same. Since the biblical text declares that the act of sex causes two to become one flesh (Genesis 2:24), the Phibionites tried to make men and women "one" as much as possible.

When the sexual acts resulted in pregnancies, thus more possibilities for creating disunity, they strategized for a "perfect Passover." The goal was to unify the unwanted child back into the people who had created it. Thus, it became rationalized as taking care of a brother's "blunder." Epiphanius writes:

They extract the fetus at the stage which is appropriate for their enterprise, take this aborted infant, and cut it up in a trough with a pestle. And they mix honey, pepper, and certain other perfumes and spices with it to keep from getting sick, and then all the revellers in this herd of swine and dogs assemble, and each eats a piece of the child with his fingers.[10]

Another Phibionite teaching was that *virginity* was defined as a woman not getting pregnant, even though she must be a constant partaker in the fornication exercises in order to be unified with as many men as possible. The Phibionites even had a formula involving the number of sexual encounters that would lead to divine status. Epiphanius spares little condemnation for the male members of this enterprise in "whoredom." With enough sexual interactions, the table of nations in Genesis could be undone and diverse people groups reunified into a divine unity. What greater gift could there be to God than to present a host of people with the primordial unity God desired?

Contemporaries of the Phibionites went to great lengths to show the sect's gross misuse of the Bible and, in this case, its gross practices as well.

IS THE BIBLE AT FAULT?

The Biblical Outcome

The Phibionites chose to focus on certain biblical texts while dismissing others and adding even more. As Gnostics, the Phibionites needed to emphasize that they were the select few who had the correct teachings. They believed the Old and New Testaments had truths in them, but those truths had become corrupted with other views that were not from God. Phibionite leaders and teachings claimed they could help members discern what was true from what was false.

The Phibionites viewed all of life through Ephesians 1:9–10, which declares that God made known "the mystery of his will . . . to unite all things in [Christ], things in heaven and things on earth." This emphasis on *mystery* and the *union of all things* was associated with Genesis 2:24, which discusses the union of male and female and the two becoming one flesh. They figured, *If 2 can become 1 through sexual intercourse, why not 3 or 4 or 730?* Moreover, if God is one (Deuteronomy 6:4) and those united with God are one with the Lord (1 Corinthians 6:17), then the Phibionites reasoned they could be united with God on the same terms as they were united with one another—hence the introduction of sexual fluids into the rite of communion. They believed they were partaking of the *stuff* of union, with God and man. The creative power bestowed on humans meant that unity came through consuming the creative fluids that God gave them, the "body" (semen) and the "blood" (menstruation). And, through this unthinkable Eucharist, all members participated in the *life* and identity of others and believed they were fulfilling the Pauline vision where there would no longer be male or female since all could be one in Christ Jesus (Galatians 3:28).

Point of Departure from Biblical Orthodoxy

The Phibionites got so far outside biblical orthodoxy that it is difficult to know where to start. The most essential departure may be the Gnostic beliefs that shaped the life of this group and led them to make claims of having special knowledge. Historic Christianity affirms Paul's claim that, "since the creation of the world God's invisible qualities—his eternal power and divine nature—have been clearly seen, being understood from what has been made, so that people are without excuse" (Romans 1:20 NIV). We don't have to join obscure groups with strange practices in search of hidden knowledge in order to know God. God makes the gospel message of salvation available to all because he does not wish "that any should perish, but that all should reach repentance" (2 Peter 3:9).

Genesis 1 presents creation as taking place through God's spoken word. And the creation of humans who could fill the earth is not presented as a problem of disunity but as a living diversity that God desires and created on purpose. So, the Gnostic attempt to lose personal identity by merging all distinctiveness is an attempt to solve a problem the Bible doesn't suggest we have.

In Christianity, the Eucharist is a sacrament. Although Christian traditions differ on how communion should be administered, there is no orthodox group that uses actual flesh or actual blood. The bread and drink of the traditional Passover feast is what Christ used, and this is the model for Christian tradition. As he broke bread at the Last Supper, Christ claimed a redemption similar to the unleavened bread and cup of redemption that was celebrated year after year in Jewish families.

The affirmation of Christian bodies being members of Christ's body does not mean sexual infidelity is permissible, as Paul makes clear in 1 Corinthians 6:15. Nor do the members need to eat semen and drink blood to be united as Christ's body. Instead, it is the act of gathering together that makes a church, and it is the church unified in faith, hope, and love that is the body of Christ.

Problem Type

Maybe the simplest way of summing up this type of interpretation is just to say that it's sloppy. It suffers from strict literalism on the one hand and, on the other, it deals in strained analogies piled on more analogies, themselves muddled by yet more analogies.

The statements about being unified with God or others were taken hyper-literally to be about a physical unity that could not be broken. In this reading, any text mentioning unity, like Ephesians or Galatians, must mean physical and sexual unity rather than unity in following God or unity in salvation from sin and death. Similarly, when Jesus refers to his body and blood at the Last Supper, this is taken as a literal reference to human bodies, which translates in the Phibionite mind to the bodily fluids we've mentioned.

The Phibionites held that Psalm 1:3's statement about a "tree planted by streams of water that yields its fruit in its season" refers to a woman's flow that can yield "fruit" when soaking up "streams." This strained interpretation is made possible by connecting the tree of life to Eve, the mother of all mankind. In their reasoning, a woman is like a tree in that she has *seasonal* menstruation that might possibly yield *fruit* twelve times a year. So, naturally, *woman equals tree*. I'm not making this up.

ANTIDOTE

The Phibionites did a lot of things wrong, but the failure of their biblical interpretation comes down to few mistakes we can learn to avoid.

First, we must remember to keep everything in context. Second, we can resist overly literal readings (especially with such gross missuses as validating sex cults). Third, we should avoid piling analogies on top of each other that inevitably warp the text. Otherwise, we end up with "Christian" practices that have nothing to do with Christ, the church, or the New Testament.

I am astonished that you are so quickly deserting him
who called you in the grace of Christ and are turning to
a different gospel—not that there is another one,
but there are some who trouble you and want to distort
the gospel of Christ. But even if we or an angel from heaven
should preach to you a gospel contrary to the one
we preached to you, let him be accursed.

GALATIANS 1:6–8

CHAPTER 3

Self-Maiming:

Why Many Have Lost More
than the Pulse of Scripture

If your right eye causes you to sin, tear it out and throw it away.
For it is better that you lose one of your members
than that your whole body be thrown into hell.
And if your right hand causes you to sin, cut it off
and throw it away. For it is better that you lose one
of your members than that your whole body go into hell.
MATTHEW 5:29–30

And [Jesus] said to all, "If anyone would come after me,
let him deny himself and take up his cross daily and follow me."
LUKE 9:23

For if you live according to the flesh you will die,
but if by the Spirit you put to death
the deeds of the body, you will live.
ROMANS 8:13

I remember talking with a classmate on the campus of Miami University in Oxford, Ohio. This conversation took place more than thirty years ago, but I remember it like it was yesterday. While discussing some archaic church practice, my friend commented, "Self-maiming isn't just something out of early church history. I know a blind pastor who followed Origen's lead and took the Bible literally. He had struggled with lust, and one night while still a young man he gouged out his eyes with a spoon." That phrase—*gouged out his eyes with a spoon*—made me queasy as he said it. Truth be told, it still does. My classmate, a conservative Christian, was helping to pastor a fundamentalist church when he personally met this blind pastor and his family.

The blind man from Ohio is now retirement age. Unfortunately, he is not alone in self-maiming actions or self-inflicted pain. Every Lenten season, the media covers reenactments of Christ's suffering, with volunteers in the Philippines experiencing crucifixion. The names of numerous participants are easily available on the web. Some are multiyear volunteers for crucifixion; at least one has participated for three decades (but obviously, unlike Christ, not unto death). Various Passion plays worldwide have some vivid imagery, and some involve self-flagellation—annually prompting discussions about "the ethics of spectacular violence."[1]

Like some of the strange customs of the Phibionites and other Gnostic sects, the act of self-maiming provides outsiders of Christian networks good reason to be suspicious of the Christian community, especially conservative Christianity. However, this is an ancient practice that predates Christianity. For example, in a text from Ugarit labeled *The Righteous Sufferer*, the speaker mentions prophets in connection with "those who bathe in their blood" via self-mutilation.[2] In addition to facilitating better prophecies, self-mutilation sometimes marked despair. Perhaps the shedding of one's own blood would demonstrate a level of seriousness to the deities.

Within Christian groups, the blind pastor from Ohio is not without historic precedent, as early church leaders debated the acceptance of self-mutilation, or *mortification*, particularly regarding self-castration to avoid the sin of lust. Justin Martyr deals with this in his mid-second-century *Apology*. There, he refers to a young Christian man who asked a Roman prefect to allow him to perform self-castration. This young man sought to counter the notion that sexual promiscuity was a secret rite among the Christians.[3] Epiphanius of Salamis, whom we quoted in the previous chapter, writes about a Transjordanian group of monks, the Valesians, who aggressively promoted self-castration—often forcing it upon new initiates. The Synod of Achaia (ca. AD 250) condemned their doctrines as heresy. Basil of Ancyra harshly disowned the growing practice in his mid-fourth-century work, *On the True Integrity of Virginity*. A generation later, John Chrysostom attacked the practice as rejecting God's created order. The Nicaean canons (AD 325) also include a general condemnation.[4] Regardless of isolated debates about who had practiced self-mortification, evidence abounds that the early church had to deal with this radical expression of faith fairly often.

The early Christians would have been aware of the frenzied ceremonies of the *Galli* (or *Galloi*), which, much like Roman rituals, had intentional purposes amid apparent pandemonium. So many Galli lived in the Roman era that Jerome comments on laws enacted to limit their numbers. The Galli were mainly self-castrated eunuchs in the service of the goddess Cybele, the famed *Magna Mater* ("Great Mother") the Romans had imported from Phrygia (ancient Turkey) to stop a plague. Arnobius of Sicca, an early Christian writer, describes the ceremonies as ghastly, disturbed affairs. Large crowds would assemble to watch as the Galli performed their rites by cutting their arms and beating each other on the back. The sounds of flutes and drums filled the air while others sang "sacred" songs. Arnobius continues:

> For while the rest are playing flutes and performing the rites, frenzy comes upon many, and many who have come simply to watch subsequently perform this act. I will describe what they do. The youth for whom these things lie in store throws off his clothes, rushes to the center with a great shout and takes up a sword. . . . He grabs it and immediately castrates himself. Then he rushes through the city holding in his hands the parts he has cut off. He takes female clothing and women's adornment from whatever house he throws these parts into. This is what they do at the Castration.[5]

Early church sources also provide problematic texts linking some Christian luminaries to the practice of self-mutilation. One was a contemporary of Bishop Polycarp and Irenaeus named Bishop Melito of Sardis in ancient Turkey. In a letter from Polycrates of Ephesus to Pope Victor (ca. AD 194), Melito is referred to as a eunuch, about fifteen years after his death.

One of the most cited and debated accounts of mortification concerns the great theologian Origen (d. ca. AD 253), who inspired my former classmate's pastor-friend to gouge out his eyes. Bishop Demetrius of Alexandria, who had grown frustrated with Origen's independence and powerful intellect, claimed that Origen was guilty of self-castration—a capital offense at the time. Eusebius's fourth-century account also seems to accuse Origen of this crime. He claims that Origen took a hyper-literal view of Matthew 19:12, "There are eunuchs who have made themselves eunuchs for the sake of the kingdom of heaven. Let the one who is able to receive this receive it." This would be surprising, given that Origen was known for his *allegorical* rather than *literal* readings of Scripture. What's more, in Origen's commentary on the same passage, he clearly orders people *not* to do so.[6] Likewise, during his two years in prison under Emperor Decius, it could be assumed that the guards would have easily discovered his condition.

Scholars remain mixed on the validity of the Origen castration scenario. Various notable scholars, including Peter Brown of Princeton University and Bill Placher of Wabash College, do not find convincing reasons to reject Eusebius's account. Eusebius, they note, seemed predisposed toward Origen with no intent on harming him. The takeaway here perhaps is not whether Origen *did* castrate himself but whether this act was practiced more widely in the church. As for Origen's case, it took on legendary proportions. Medieval illuminated manuscripts capture Origen's bold move with "strangely disturbing" images.[7] Perhaps none is more curious than the fourteenth-century French miniature "Origen Castrating Himself before a Nun."[8] Whether Origen did or didn't, the point to remember here is that many Christian leaders *did* harm themselves in this way. For example, Theodoret claims that Leontius, an Arian bishop of Antioch, had been deposed after being accused of self-castration.[9]

Castration was not the only form of self-mutilation, though. In the twelfth century, accounts arose of nuns who disfigured themselves to repulse potential assailants. One such nun, St. Ebba, urged her sisters to cut off their noses or upper lips so that Vikings approaching the convent would not find them attractive.[10]

In recent years, we have vivid and full-color reminders of the concept of self-inflicted pain for religious reasons, commonly called self-flagellation. The Brotherhood of Canindezinho in Brazil retains an active membership; they ritualistically cut themselves with razors tied to strings—especially on their backs.[11] Perhaps this curious concept is most famously portrayed in Dan Brown's novel *The Da Vinci Code*, a best-selling and controversial thriller (2003). Ron Howard's movie version of this book presents a haunting representation of the book's albino Catholic monk, Silas, living out corporal (body) mortification. The film, which claimed more than $750 million in ticket sales, sensationalized the practice and put it on display for a wide audience of moviegoers. In the wave of inquiries and interviews that resulted, the staff of the Roman Catholic Opus Dei organization both clarified and endorsed aspects of this practice.[12] The BBC News followed up on this theme, reporting a mixed response. Some scholars, such as Catholic historian Michael Walsh, believe corporal mortification has disappeared among Catholic priests and monks. "Early Christians thought the body was evil and needed to be controlled," he said. "Quite simply, we now have a greater understanding that such practices are not healthy."[13] But others, like Professor Lewis Ayres of Durham University, believe a "tiny minority" within the more conservative Catholic orders still practice it. Opus Dei's Andrew Soane, like others from Opus Dei in filmed interviews on its own homepage, attests to some version of corporal mortification's persistence. "It may happen that this change is reversed as people reconnect with their bodies and take control via moderate fasting and some corporal mortification, finding it a very healthy practice, which can overcome such unhealthy developments as drug use, sexual addictions, eating disorders and other body-hating approaches."[14]

All these Christian groups, from the second century to the present, may intend to show commitment to Christ in an intense manner, and to "partake in his sufferings" (see 1 Peter 4:13; Philippians 3:10). For those during the Roman era, perhaps they did not want to be outdone by pagan priests. Sometimes the motivation stemmed from earnest desires to fulfill biblical texts and avoid lust or the accusation of lust. Regardless of the reasons for self-inflicted pain and mutilation, often from what we know otherwise to be pious individuals, the acts appear counter to the New Testament's message—which calls us to focus on the heart and the mind and trust a benevolent and omniscient God who knows the status of both.

IS THE BIBLE AT FAULT?

The Biblical Outcome

The use of biblical texts to support self-mutilation is based on a hyper-literal interpretation of four main texts:

- Matthew 19:12, which mentions making oneself a eunuch for the kingdom of heaven. When taken literally, this passage elevates those who commit self-castration for the sake of the kingdom.
- Matthew 18:8–9, in which Jesus urges the avoidance of sin even if it means cutting off an arm or gouging out an eye. When taken literally, this passage legitimizes self-mutilation.
- 1 Corinthians 9:27, in which Paul declares, "I discipline my body and keep it under control." Here some readers infer that Paul is literally beating his body into submission, resulting in self-induced harm. This act of self-harm is viewed as model behavior after Paul's exhortation to readers to imitate what they have seen him do (Philippians 4:9).
- Romans 8:13, which appears to promote the concept of mortification in Paul's encouragement to "put to death the misdeeds of the body" (NIV) or to "mortify the deeds of the body" (KJV). Although most Christians would read this verse as an exhortation to subjugate their sinful natures, those advocating self-mutilation read here a reference to killing the flesh in a literal sense, to enable or facilitate living by the Spirit.

Hyper-literal interpretation of Scripture can lead to rather problematic and often untenable marching orders. Fortunately, most seminaries help preachers see the error of this hermeneutic.

Point of Departure from Biblical Orthodoxy

Responsible readings of these passages are grounded in the broader biblical history of God's creation of our physical bodies and his desire that we use these bodies in service of his kingdom. The idea that God would ask us to mutilate or abuse our bodies also goes against trust in God regardless of circumstances (Philippians 4:12). If Christians grant God the power to give or take life, they also relinquish their bodies to divine guidance. In many of the instances of self-harm we've examined, we see nothing that furthers the kingdom of God. Instead, these acts seem to improve the status of the perpetrator. Therefore, these are not kingdom-oriented acts; they're not serving God or the gospel. They subvert God's calling on our lives or present impossible standards that go against God's hope for humanity. For just one example, the divine command to be "fruitful and multiply" (Genesis 1:28) would have been impossible if the ones who received the command in Genesis chose self-castration.

Additionally, all these Christians who inflicted self-maiming had a biblical backdrop that warns against such things, such as 1 Kings 18:24–29, Leviticus 19:28, and Mark 5:2–5. Let's take a closer look at these three passages.

In 1 Kings 18:24–29, the prophets of Baal perform acts of self-mutilation in order to get their god's attention, but it yields no result in the story. In fact, Elijah's simple prayer to Jehovah (Lord) a few verses later yields the very result the mutilation of the prophets failed to produce.

In Leviticus 19:28, we're told the act of grieving for a deceased loved one should not lead the mourner to cut oneself or mark the body. This kind of cutting and marking was common to some of Israel's neighbors, who used it as a way of declaring that the gods had made a mistake. It was a message to the gods that they needed to restore the deceased loved one or else the griever would continue this type of self-harm. In Israel, this was an impious act that was denounced on the grounds that the people were to trust God in life or death.

In Mark 5:2–5, self-mutilation is the result of demon possession, as the man from "the tombs" with the "unclean spirit" cut himself with stones. "Legion," the many demons that possessed this man, were trying to harm their host in every way possible. In casting out the demons, Jesus restored the man and put an end to his self-harm.

The church took this matter seriously throughout history. In fact, the orthodox church's condemnation of the practice of self-harm was so great that one ancient pope, Pope Gelasius I (AD 492–496), declared that priests who self-castrated would be relieved of their priestly duties.[15]

Problem Type

Some of the problems with self-castration lie simply in damaging or limiting the bodies God gave us. And, in one sense, self-mutilation is a form of self-hatred and denial of our created selves. Even when the case is made that self-castration would display fidelity or further the kingdom or deter criticism, it is the *self* in self-castration that is problematic. The same is true for self-mutilation. The act of maiming oneself is *destructive* of oneself. Even in the times when it may appear a means of deterring dangerous or violent behavior, these acts rule out divine intervention through miracles or displays of faithfulness and love in the midst of persecution. And, even when they are intended to prevent pain or sin, there's no guarantee that they work (such as the case of violent sexual crimes). This is a debate beyond the scope of this book, but linked to the rationale one uses to process these questions. The self-maiming of the nuns under St. Ebba resulted in the burning down of the convent with the nuns inside because the Vikings burned things that disgusted them.

Furthermore, as with a lot of these misuses and abuses, some of the problems with biblical arguments for self-maiming come from taking statements hyper-literally and taking them out of context— two exegetical errors that usually take us further from the true meaning of the texts in question.

ANTIDOTE

For the texts in Matthew, the contexts of the statements are important to consider. Matthew 18 is a good example. It begins by Jesus declaring that members of the kingdom must receive it like a child who is dependent upon a parent's provisions. As Jesus is encouraging vulnerability, he's saying that those who would abuse this dependence on guidance would do better to be drowned than to mislead others to their own destruction. It's in this context that Jesus declares that if your hands or feet or eyes cause a scandal, which in the Greek *skandalizo* means to cause another to stumble, then it is better to burn them. The focus is on misleading others who depend on you. Causing another to stumble is a serious offense in the New Testament, and Jesus is saying that it would be better to lose a part of your body than to cause someone else to lose their soul.

In many regards, Paul demonstrates this idea in Galatians 5:12 with his comments against those who claim circumcision is necessary for salvation. Paul disagrees with this view and considers it an attempt to mislead people and keep them from accepting the true gospel message. Therefore, Paul is saying that, if they are going to remove some of their skin (foreskin), they might as well go the whole way and cut off the whole apparatus it's attached to. He's frustrated, and he's essentially making a dark joke here. This is not advice for believers; it's a jab at his opponents.

The next passage, Matthew 19:12, yields similar results. Some translations seem to go along with the interpretation of self-mutilators. The ESV reads, "For there are eunuchs who have been so from birth, and there are eunuchs who have been made eunuchs by men, and there are eunuchs who have made themselves eunuchs for the sake of the kingdom of heaven. Let the one who is able to receive this receive it." Other translations give more perspective for the sense of the text. The NIV says, "And there are those who choose to live like eunuchs for the sake of the kingdom of heaven." The New Living Translation reads, "And some choose not to marry for the sake of the Kingdom of Heaven." These translations provide a better sense of the meaning of *eunuch* in this context. This is not a reference to self-castration in a literal sense. Rather, Jesus declares these people have accepted the kingdom of heaven and devoted themselves to further the interests of the kingdom rather than getting married or trying to produce children.

Paul's comment in 1 Corinthians 9:27 benefits from context as well. In this chapter, he compares his actions to a runner who subjects his body to training. He talks about subduing his body and disciplining it. He's not talking about maiming himself but about training his body in order to use it more effectively. We see the same thing in Romans 8:13, where Paul says laws won't ensure godly living, nor will choosing to indulge the desires of one's flesh. Living by the Spirit, though, can end or "kill" the evil actions that one's flesh desires. Paul is not declaring that *members* (parts) of the body need to die but rather the *deeds* of that body that are motivated by fleshly desires.

Psalm 139 is one of many scriptures that makes clear that God creates us all special, and our uniqueness is established when he knits us together before birth. An oft-quoted Scripture is, "I am fearfully and wonderfully made" (v. 14). If we are praising God for how he made us, it is logical that altering his creation detracts from that sense of appreciation and praise.

For you formed my inward parts; you knitted me together
in my mother's womb. I praise you, for I am fearfully
and wonderfully made. Wonderful are your works;
my soul knows it very well.
PSALM 139:13–14

Or do you not know that your body is a temple
of the Holy Spirit within you, whom you have from God?
You are not your own, for you were bought with a price.
So glorify God in your body.
1 CORINTHIANS 6:19–20

CHAPTER 4

Mishandling Scripture:

How Handling Snakes Comes Back to Bite You

And he said to them, "Go into all the world and proclaim
the gospel to the whole creation. Whoever believes
and is baptized will be saved, but whoever does not believe
will be condemned. And these signs will accompany
those who believe: in my name they will cast out demons;
they will speak in new tongues; they will pick up serpents
with their hands; and if they drink any deadly poison,
it will not hurt them; they will lay their hands
on the sick, and they will recover."

MARK 16:15–18

Pastors of around one hundred and twenty-five American churches have at least two things in common with Adam and Eve (besides being fallen creatures): they do not shy away from snakes and are not worried about their bite. In recent history, however, many of these pastors and some of their parishioners have had abrupt—and surprising—venomous ends. Taking Mark 16:18 literally, they've picked up serpents. Sometimes the same snake they had handled hundreds of times caused their excruciating deaths.

Pastor Jamie Coots was a living legend in Middlesboro, Kentucky—at least among his twenty church members. He and his eldest son, Cody, represent four generations of snake handlers and a longer line of modern snake handlers that trace their roots to Dolly Pond Church of God in Birchwood, Tennessee, founded around 1909. In its heyday, the movement boasted several thousand practitioners, found mainly in remote Appalachian churches.

Pastor Coots survived nine snakebites up through 2013, each one garnering him credibility among his small circle. Every time he raised his right hand in praise, they saw evidence of his journey: a snake bite had cost him his middle finger. The finger withered away for days after the bite until it eventually fell off. In a televised interview for ABC News's *Nightline* program in 2013, Coots boldly displayed his dead, detached finger. His wife had collected it from their front yard, saying, "I'll always have a piece of you no matter where you go."[1]

His wife's gesture foreshadowed the inevitable. During a Saturday night church meeting soon after, in February 2014, a rattlesnake bit Pastor Coots on the hand. An EMS arrived at 8:30 p.m., but he refused treatment and went home. At 9:10 p.m., the EMS arrived at his house, but his wife signed a medical release form rejecting help. He died within the hour at age forty-two. Fangs cut short the life of a second Reverend Coots; sadly, his father had died the same way.[2]

Another pastor was present during Coots's fatal finale: his young apprentice, Andrew Hamblin of the Tabernacle Church of God in LaFollette, Tennessee. Hamblin had a prominent role in the sixteen–part National Geographic reality series, *Snake Salvation*.[3] He still sees himself and his flock as "just like any other Christian" and is forthright about his main desire, which is to see people saved through the blood of Jesus.[4] His TV time prompted local authorities to remove fifty poisonous snakes from his church due to laws prohibiting ownership of dangerous animals. Ironically, the law was enacted in 1947 after five worshipers died of snakebites.

In a news conference, Hamblin said, "If God moves on me and I feel led through him by the Holy Ghost to reach my arm into a box of rattlesnakes, I should have my religious right to do that." Hamblin admits that snake handling is not tied to an essential salvation doctrine. "I'm not asking anyone to agree with me or believe like me," he said. "I've never told anybody that they need to take up serpents to go to heaven, to be a Christian."[5] If it's not an "essential salvation doctrine," then one might ask why he risks his life every week doing it.

Two years before Jamie Coots's death, Pastor Mack Wolford died in West Virginia from a timber rattler that struck his thigh during an outdoor service. He was only forty-four and had survived previous bites. He had also drunk strychnine several times. He, like Pastor Jamie Coots and now Cody Coots, had watched his father die from a snakebite during a church service. Mack Wolford had been only fifteen; his father, thirty-nine.

Like Coots, Mack Wolford had been part of major media coverage the year before his own fatal bite. Journalist Julia Duin captures his role in the annual Labor Day homecoming at West Virginia's Jolo Church of the Lord Jesus.[6] She puts this in context clearly, noting that mainline Pentecostal movements condemn snake handling. The sad irony of this particular gathering spot at Jolo, founded in 1956 by Bob and Barbara Elkins, is that Barbara's daughter from a previous marriage died of a snakebite in 1961 at the age of twenty-three. Witnesses attest to packed services before the incident. By 2017, though, only a dozen or so members attended regularly, most battling severe drug addictions. A hand-lettered statement taped near the pulpit reads: "The pastor and congregation are not responsible for anyone that handles the serpents and gets bit. If you get bit, the church will stand by you and pray with you. And the same goes with drinking the poison."[7]

Ironically, the leader of the Jolo annual homecoming at the Church of the Lord Jesus in West Virginia is a gravedigger. He told the reporter he was worried about the lack of teens attending—implying fear for the movement's future. The creators of popular television show *The Simpsons* parody the combination of novelty and horror well with Moe Szyslak's vintage dialogue in "Eeny Teeny Maya Moe," in which he claims to be a nonpracticing snake handler out of respect for his father.[8]

To many Christians, snake handling seems about as bizarre a religious practice as one could imagine in modern times, especially considering the number of deaths that have occurred as a result. Yet historic statements reveal it once attracted thousands of practitioners, making this American phenomenon all the more curious.

In some ways, the movement has come full circle. The pastor credited with founding the Dolly Pond Church of God in East Tennessee around 1909, George Went Hensley, died of a snakebite in 1955 in Florida. Unlike Pastor Coots, he had preached this practice as evidence of salvation, making his death problematic for his followers who would then have to question the salvation of their founder. Though Hensley started a movement that attracted a surprising number of participants, the ritual's survival is in jeopardy as long as celebrity pastors like Coots and Wolford can't even outlive their snakes.

IS THE BIBLE AT FAULT?

The Biblical Outcome

The Scripture passage cited most often by snake-handling ministries is Mark 16:17–18. Here, Jesus informs his disciples that one sign of belief in the spreading of the gospel will be the ability to pick up poisonous snakes and drink poison without being harmed. Modern snake handlers, including the Cootses and Andrew Hamblin, take this passage literally and apply it to themselves.

In addition to the Mark passage, Acts 28:3–6 factors into this discussion. This passage shows the apostle Paul shipwrecked on the island of Malta, where he survived a venomous snakebite unharmed, much to the amazement of the Maltese. Snake-handling ministries focus on the conversion of this island following Paul's snakebite and treat it as a model for evangelism. If Paul converted an entire island with the help of a poisonous snake, why shouldn't we do the same today? Following this line of thought, snake handling is a public practice, performed in front of church audiences and sometimes on television, so that people can see the divine protection of Jesus and put their faith in him as well.

Point of Departure from Biblical Orthodoxy

Mark 16:17–18 is part of a larger selection (Mark 16:9–20) that many scholars consider a late addition to the end of Mark. The authority of this passage is widely debated due to its absence in many of the earliest surviving manuscripts of Mark's Gospel. Many books and articles have been devoted to this passage and some provide helpful lists of the wide array of authors for and against the inclusion of this text in the official biblical canon.[9]

Those who oppose the authority of Mark 16:9–20 view this passage as a later addition that summarizes the resurrection appearances found in the other Gospels and Acts. This view highlights the fact that the earliest two versions of Mark, from Codex Vaticanus and Codex Sinaiticus, do not include these verses. Likewise, leading church writers in the third century, Clement of Alexandria and Origen, don't mention these verses among their voluminous writings and translations. Bruce Metzger, an eminent Greek scholar from Princeton, also notes that Jerome and Eusebius perceive the section to be absent from nearly all the copies of Mark known at that time. Also, Ammonius does not include the questionable passage in his *Diatessaron-Gospel,* which informed the later Eusebian canon tables. These Ammonian sections and canon tables established scholarship of the Gospels for cross-referencing passages. They also informed Origen's massive *Hexapla* a century later.[10]

Those who accept the authority of Mark 16:9–20 challenge these claims. One of these scholars contends that "Justin, Tatian, the unknown author of *Epistula Apostolorum,* and Irenaeus, from the 100's [second century]—all of whom utilized the contents of Mark 16:9–20 in one way or another. Also, Codex Vaticanus' copyist left a distinct blank space after Mark 16:8, indicating his awareness of the absent verses."[11] Traditions today hold that viewing Mark 16:9–20 as part of the canon avoids what is seen to be an abrupt ending to Mark where the women run from the tomb in fear without saying anything.

But the inclusion or exclusion of Mark 16:9–20 is not the sole determining factor for how we as Christians should approach the issue of snake handling. Orthodox Christianity does not condone putting one's life at risk unnecessarily or putting the lives of others at risk. In fact, Romans 13:10 declares that love does not cause harm to a neighbor. On the contrary, Proverbs 6:16–19 declares that God detests hands that spill innocent blood and one who sows discord among brothers, both of which can be applied to communities who lose members and ministers to death by snakebite. Moreover, Christians affirm the value of medical treatment, as when James invites the one who is sick to receive both oil and prayer (James 5:14). The application of figs to Hezekiah's boil in Isaiah 38:21 is another example of the place of medicine in fulfilling God's declarations of healing.

Problem Type

However we view the authority of Mark 16:9–20, reading this passage as an encouragement to handle poisonous snakes is an example of hyper-literal interpretation. The signs mentioned in Mark 16:9–20 are mentioned as being spoken directly to the disciples by Jesus. Each of these signs appears in the book of Acts and confirms the gospel message that the disciples have been given to deliver, as we hear in Mark 16:20. There's no indication in the text that Jesus's message to the disciples is intended for anyone beyond his immediate audience.

Assuming that everything Jesus asks of his disciples is also requested of us today opens a wider exegetical problem. Should we all wait in Jerusalem until the Holy Spirit comes? Should we travel to meet Jesus in Galilee? The passage in Acts appears alongside the mention of demons and sickness, and a hyper-literal reading of this passage would require us to seek out demons to bring into the church so that belief could be displayed.

And, as we've seen with other misreadings, there is a shift in emphasis with snake handling that takes our focus away from God and onto the handlers themselves. Unlike Paul, who did not actively seek out a snake, the snake handlers purposefully grab snakes to make a point to a crowd. Because of this, the sign that is given is not that Jesus has power over forces of evil such as demons, snakes, poison, and sickness but rather that the speaker, or handler, has great faith. This shift in focus is evident in the folk-celebrity status that many handlers achieve, and the disproportionate attention that this one performance has in the wider scope of their ministry. Becoming preoccupied with our personal performance or boldness can lead to our losing sight of the gospel and becoming reckless with our own lives and the lives of others.

ANTIDOTE

Again, context is crucial to getting the Bible right. In the case of Mark 16:9–20, it is important to note that verse 15 instructs the disciples to preach the gospel to "the whole creation." If taken literally, the word for creation includes the seas and animals and rocks and trees. Very few would take such a statement literally enough to go into the woods to try to convert rocks and trees to the Christian faith. There must be some expectation of common sense in the way we read these passages.

The point of Mark 16:9–20, as well as the context for the snake-handling passage in verses 17–18, is that Jesus can help those in doubt by demonstrating lordship over forces of evil such as demons, snakes, poison, and sickness. These kinds of demonstrations have already happened in Acts and are sufficient for us today. It's also worth noting that Mark 16:20 places the initiative and confirmation of these signs with the Lord and *not* with a process that depends on human performance.

Even beyond the issues of context, snake handlers have problems with the wording of Mark 16:17–18 in the original language. The order of the Greek text is problematic because verse 17 says, "And these signs will accompany those who believe." Notice that the signs are not to unbelievers, but believers; the signs are *received* by believers, not *performed by* them for the benefit of nonbelievers. Additionally, there is ambiguity in the way Mark 16:18 describes picking up the snakes. Verse 18 uses a masculine plural noun for snakes and a masculine plural verb for raising, which could mean either "they will raise up snakes" *or* "snakes will raise (themselves) up."

The reference to poison in the second part of verse 18 is equally ambiguous. The precise wording literally reads, "if fatal is something they drink it will certainly not harm them." The translators of the English Standard Version offer, "and if they drink any deadly poison, it will not hurt them . . ." The New International Version translators offer, "and when they drink deadly poison, it will not hurt them at all."

It should be noted that, while interpreters may connect the raised serpents to not being harmed, the "if" in the original Greek means that the raised snakes could be independent of, and unrelated to, both the presence of poison and the phrase about "not being harmed." So it's possible that the snakes referred to are not "poisonous," and that the clause about not being harmed applies only to the drinking of poison, not to the handling of snakes. Either way, there is no suggestion that handling snakes or drinking poison is something the disciples are encouraged actively to pursue.

Against this backdrop, the Appalachian snake-handling churches, for many—especially mainstream media—defy logic, if not traditional readings of the Mark ending. The irony of all of this steps forward in the *Wall Street Journal.* Journalist Julia Duin, already cited here for other articles on this religious tradition, gives us a rather provocative article, "Christian Serpent-Handlers Protect Us All: We enjoy religious freedom because of those who hold unpopular beliefs." She notes, "Some Americans attend church every Sunday not knowing if they're going to make it out alive. . . . These believers choose to bring venomous snakes to their houses of worship." Unlike earlier articles by various writers, she notes an uptick of youth involved. "A lot of the handlers are young folks who post videos on Facebook, with captions like 'Holiness by choice, saved by grace, believer and doer of the five Bible signs.'" In light of our above discussion, it is interesting that she qualifies her assessment: "The exact timing and origin of the text doesn't matter to these believers. It's in the Bible now, and they see all five signs as mandated practices. Keeping them alive is an important Gospel truth to them and a sign of God's power."[12]

Duin brings to the forefront another complexity—the constitutional rights of what the majority of Christians likely categorize as bizarre and irresponsible behavior. Or, the general public for that matter. She argues:

> The First Amendment was made for believers such as these. In this era of debates over the rights of florists and cake-shop owners, these folks are willing to die for their unpopular beliefs. Whether it's the Amish, the Adventists or the Appalachian snake handlers, it's the people on the margins who protect the rest of us.

In the end, however, no matter how likeable some of these individuals are—like many of the protagonists here—we look to make decisions on principle not personality. On the constitutional front, she makes that very shift as well.[13]

While the layers of complexity seem to keep building around

such practices, embracing and protecting Christian orthodoxy demands we revert to the text and its context within the greater New Testament corpus. The ending of Mark is an altogether complicated text that fails to support the practice of snake handling on a number of levels. We're reminded of the importance of careful reading, especially when dealing with something so dangerous as this—or something so entertaining for outsiders as the Dolly Pond Church of God.

For the time is coming when people will not endure sound
teaching, but having itching ears they will accumulate
for themselves teachers to suit their own passions,
and will turn away from listening to the truth
and wander off into myths.

2 TIMOTHY 4:3–4

CHAPTER 5

Misguided Media Messengers:

Trading False Prophecy for Temporary Profits

But false prophets also arose among the people,
just as there will be false teachers among you, who will
secretly bring in destructive heresies, even denying
the Master who bought them. . . . And in their greed
they will exploit you with false words.
Their condemnation from long ago is not idle,
and their destruction is not asleep.

2 PETER 2:1, 3

C hristmas was canceled—at least for a group of Detroit parishioners. Instead, Christmas had been replaced with Philamathyu, an eight-day party that began on the birthday of their spiritual leader, James Francis Marion Jones—or "Prophet Jones," as he was known. He sat in front of the crowd in his self-designed, towering, arched, velvet-pleated canopy on stage. The crimson and gold throne cost $12,000 in the 1950s, and the pastor's intention was to make himself look like Solomon. He claimed messianic powers, and he issued wide-ranging prophecies during each Philamathyu. According to one of those prophecies, death and labor were to come to an end by 2000. I guess we're safe on that one.

Perhaps his most acclaimed prophecy was that Dwight D. Eisenhower (Republican) would win the 1952 presidential election. When Eisenhower won in a landslide (55.2 percent of the popular vote, 442 electoral votes, and 39 states), Prophet Jones received an invitation to the inauguration. He was in the national limelight. During his heyday, he boasted about having 2 million followers at more than 400 centers nationwide (generally considered now an exaggeration intended to fuel his image). What is verifiable: 2,500 people had once packed into his main meeting place at Detroit's refurbished Oriole Theater at Linwood near Virginia Park.

The wealthy prophet, who owned more than four hundred suits, accepted generous gifts from his followers (that they charged on credit). Many parishioners lived on the brink of poverty while he strutted in his white mink overcoat, ate off gold plates, had a full-time seamstress, and traveled in a fleet of five Cadillacs—each with a chauffeur. It is indeed a bizarre-but-true tale with a tragic ending.

This is the story of the "Messiah in Mink," as the *Saturday Evening Post* dubs him, and his "Dominionite" followers. Prophet Jones incorporated the Church of Universal Triumph, Dominion of God in Detroit in 1938. It is officially categorized, according to its adherents, not as a *church* but a *kingdom*. They are not *church members* but registered *citizens*. He began this so-called kingdom after he broke from his former mother church in Birmingham, Alabama, after a disagreement about the gifts he'd received from his *citizens*. The deacons of Birmingham's Triumph the Church and Kingdom of God in Christ, which had originally sent him to Michigan as a missionary, claimed that the expensive gifts were rightfully the property of the sending church—a standard practice for most religious and secular organizations.

Beyond the opulence was the list of proclamations and taboos. Since many believed he was a vessel on earth in which God himself was residing and that heaven would soon come to earth (the year 2000, according to Prophet Jones), they followed him. He preached five to six hours at a time, during services that began around 10:00 p.m. and lasted until around 4:00 a.m., so it would take several volumes to catalogue all his statements. The *Detroit News* summarizes his practices in its 1997 feature "Detroit's Flamboyant Prophet Jones."[1] It reads,

The only way to succeed, the prophet warned, was to obey his approximately fifty decrees. For example, "No citizen must be the father or mother of a illegitimate child." And, "women should wear girdles, long enough to keep the stomach and buttocks from protruding." Men must wear "health belts, or short stomach girdles." He wanted women to wear clear nail polish for day, and red for evening. "Steam baths should be taken often, a laxative once or twice a week."[2]

For his local Detroit audience, Richard Bak provides a lengthy reflection on Prophet Jones in *Hour Detroit* (2016), with a telling subtitle: "Before a sex scandal brought him down, the 'Messiah in Mink' was one of the more prominent black celebrity preachers of midcentury America." The other two key preachers in this category, according to Bak, were Father Divine and Sweet Daddy Grace. It seems a bit ominous being placed in the company of orators like Father Divine, who launched the International Peace Mission movement, but also claimed to be God—Jesus Christ reborn (and took the name Reverend Major Jealous Divine). According to Bak, Prophet Jones's lifestyle seemed to be positioned as public proof of his own divine appointment. He flaunted it, giving the media tours of his fifty-four-room manse at 75 Arden Park near today's Boston-Edison Historic District. Besides quoting the price of his furnishings to visitors, he held most business meetings with non-Dominion members in a small room with a perpetually burning fireplace (which he alleged was divinely ordered) and a life-size picture of himself. Bak reports, "Jones always went first class. When he visited Father Divine in New York, he brought along four valets, four bodyguards, three secretaries, his housekeeper, a hairdresser, three musicians, 60 singers, a personal cook, and a dietitian."[3]

Life magazine commits several pages to the prophet but not for his biblical teaching or humanitarian deeds. Rather, the piece emphasizes—and the article is even titled—"Prophet's Mink." Nine pictures appear of Pastor Jones wearing his $12,900 fur coat made from 75 rare pelts with a gold-handled cane over the left sleeve. The Jackson sisters, who were public school teachers, gave him the coat and other gifts (including a bracelet adorned with 812 diamonds). They believed he had healed one sister's goiter and asked him to heal their mother. "His treatment: take the mother to the Gary, [Indiana] bus station four times, make her swallow water from the washroom tap."[4] He renamed the grateful sisters Princesses Essentina (Esther) and Bluntella (Evelyn), which may have made them feel a little better about their $475 monthly payments on the mink.

According to *Jet* magazine, the Open Door Church of Holiness in Detroit posthumously named him "Patron Saint of Prosperity," a fitting canonized moniker. Rev. Jesse Irwin, Jr. has noted a spiritual reason for canonizing him. He claims that Prophet Jones spoke to the leaders of Open Door Church of Holiness from the afterlife, helping them find a new location for their church, which had recently burned. However, others ascribe his *prosperity* canonization to unique fundraising practices. He was known to shake down his parishioners for cash gifts, sometimes locking the Oriole Theater doors until he got enough in his offerings. According to attendees, these were run somewhat like auctions or public pledges—but with actual cash. Pastor Jones would ask for $20, $10, or $5 bills to be placed on a tarp in front of his throne, with the obedient ones stepping forward then allowed to leave. At last resort, he asked for $3 at minimum, ordering his citizens at least to offer support for the three parts of the Trinity. "'Now, I know the rest of you can at least afford $3. I'm asking for $3—one for the Father, one for the Son, and one for the Holy Ghost.'"[5] It is difficult not to be prosperous when twenty-five thousand worshipers are pressured to give in such a manner or be unable to leave an all-night service. Knowing many people gambled, he also sold a series of numbers for the lottery, and he resold pictures of himself that had appeared in local papers, asking several times the price of the newspaper but offering his special blessing.

The latter part of Prophet Jones's "ministry" was marred with a national sex scandal that cost him much of his popularity and revenue streams. As we saw with the Israelite House of David scandal and with various other celebrity religious figures, Prophet Jones was caught in the same improper sexual situations he constantly preached against. In 1953, one of his male valets was caught propositioning a male undercover police officer in a downtown men's room. The judge ordered the valet to leave the prophet's mansion. Then, in 1956, the police raided Jones's mansion to investigate "morals charges" and found the prophet in his pajamas with two teen boys. He claimed he was giving them music lessons. The raid was prompted by an incident two weeks earlier, in which Prophet Jones allegedly propositioned James A. Henry, a member of the Vice Bureau. At the time, in addition to the issues with minors, same-sex relations were considered criminal.

After the six-day trial, the jury acquitted Prophet Jones of gross indecency charges, but his reputation was severely tarnished. He exited the courtroom to "cheering crowds" that yelled his mantra, "All is well!" Jones proclaimed, "I have won my fight with the devil. Now I am going to launch a nation-wide crusade to save souls."[6]

Failure to launch is more apropos, as he lost too much of his following and income and had to sell his mansion. He eventually found his small traveling entourage stranded in St. Louis and in ensuing months became entangled in criminal allegations. A convicted robber of a Maryland bank implicated Prophet Jones, claiming that Jones convinced (the police said *bewitched*) the bank janitor to turn over the keys to the robber.[7] Though again acquitted, he had lost his mesmerizing influence over large crowds of seekers and givers. For some scholars, part of his appeal wasn't actually the spiritual answers, but his understanding of those who felt oppressed. While he prophesied that labor would vanish in the year 2000 and strutted his elite lifestyle, he was also giving hope to urban minorities. "From the [Detroit

Industrial Mission's] perspective, Jones would have appeared a flim-flam artist; yet he was communicating important, affirming messages that the black working class needed to hear."[8]

Prophet Jones died in 1971 as his influence and appeal continued to diminish. However, fifteen thousand people gathered to pay their respects—the last gift they had to offer the charismatic leader. A closing irony of Prophet Jones's life was the location of his funeral service, the Adlai Stevenson Building Auditorium on Grand River. In attendance were representatives from some two dozen of the congregations (similar to churches) claiming allegiance to the Church of Universal Triumph, Dominion of God which Prophet Jones founded.

The Dominion "church" still meets today, though far from the media stage of its founding voice. It claims thirty-five branches (or "thankful centers"), schools, and seminaries, and remains head-quartered in Detroit.

IS THE BIBLE AT FAULT?

The Biblical Outcome

As strange as this movement is, it has important connections with biblical themes and passages that should not be overlooked. Most obviously, Prophet Jones declared that he was preaching the true gospel. He claimed to be a prophet, the Messiah, and the fulfillment of Christ's second coming. He claimed to perform signs of the kingdom that included healing, preaching, blessing, condemning, and prophesying.

Among the biblical passages Jones used to establish his church were Amos 3:7, Matthew 6:9–13, Revelation 11:15, and Revelation 21:1–5. Each of these passages connects to an aspect of his alleged prophetic ministry:

- Amos 3:7 mentions God revealing secrets to prophets.
- Mathew 6:9–13 offers the prayer that God's kingdom would come and God's will would be done on earth as in heaven; also present is the request for bread and deliverance from evil.
- Revelation 11:15 proclaims the kingdom of the world would become the kingdom of Christ that will last forever.
- Revelation 21:1–5 describes a New Jerusalem where God dwells and wipes away tears, ends death, and removes pain.

In claiming to be Messiah, Jones promised each of these passages about the kingdom was coming true in or through him.

Point of Departure from Biblical Orthodoxy

If we ran a timeline from the fall of the Jewish Temple in AD 70 to today, every generation would have a bizarre story about a minister, priest, monk, or pastor. Few in the modern era would be more flamboyant and radically opulent than Detroit's Reverend James Francis Marion Jones. His uniqueness is less in his distortion and manipulation of biblical truths than in his colorful life and teachings. He offers an ideal case study of what the lure of greed and prestige can do to our reading of the Bible.

Linking his teaching with any orthodox tradition is clearly problematic. The simplest biblical rejection of Prophet Jones's behavior is the well-known adage that one cannot serve both God and money (Matthew 6:24). In fact, the Bible insists that the kingdom of God requires that God alone be deemed the king. As king, God devotes special attention to the poor and to making sure the impoverished get justice. Those who deprive the poor of what they need are opposed by God, who is powerful enough to overthrow any unjust leader or group of people. Rather than living with a focus on self, orthodox biblical ethics encourage us to live out selfless love in acts of charity as the servants of all. It would be difficult to describe Prophet Jones's ministry this way.

Problem Type

Prophet Jones's biggest problem may have been in his application of biblical themes without the ethics of love that accompany them. His use of Amos is especially ironic, as one of the core messages of this book is the prophet's criticism of those who are at ease in their riches while depriving the poor of what they need to survive. Amos 6:1–7 warns:

> Woe to you . . . [who] lie on beds adorned with ivory and lounge on your couches. You dine on choice lambs and

fattened calves. You strum away on your harps like David and improvise on musical instruments. You drink wine by the bowlful and use the finest lotions, but you do not grieve over the ruin of Joseph. Therefore you will be among the first to go into exile; your feasting and lounging will end. (NIV)

A similar economic dynamic can be found in Revelation 18:3, which identifies wickedness in Babylon that leads the nations astray from God's instructions—kings and leaders commit immoral acts and grew rich from the power of luxury. The prophetic voice heard in Revelation 18:4–8 urges the faithful to cease residing with these people who glorify themselves, because the Lord will bring torment and mourning to them.

Am I saying God wants us all to live in poverty and give everything we have away? No, not necessarily. Some may be so called. Others, for various reasons, have extreme wealth. There are strong Christians in both camps. But the spirit of Prophet Jones's decisions places his lifestyle in obvious conflict with many biblical claims about the kingdom of God. His issue became his apparent preoccupation with possessions, not the possessions themselves.

Perhaps Prophet Jones's most problematic claim is that of him being the returned (second coming of) Christ. Jesus warns against such people in Matthew 24:23–27:

Then if anyone says to you, "Look, here is the Christ!" or "There he is!" do not believe it. For false christs and false prophets will arise and perform great signs and wonders, so as to lead astray, if possible, even the elect. See, I have told you beforehand. So, if they say to you, "Look, he is in the wilderness," do not go out. If they say, "Look, he is in the inner rooms," do not believe it. For as the lightning comes from the east and shines as far as the west, so will be the coming of the Son of Man.

The mark of the true Christ is a swift arrival that cannot be missed. And the mark of a true messiah is one whose humanity permits familiarity with pain and suffering and death because of his willingness to take on the pain and suffering and death of others.

ANTIDOTE

The antidote to these lavish abuses is the life of Christ. Christ was born into a poor family that could not find a place to stay. The trajectory of Christ's life was one of homeless service to people without thought of gain or reward. Instead, Christ "emptied himself, by taking the form of a servant, being born in the likeness of men. And being found in human form, he humbled himself by becoming obedient to the point of death, even death on a cross" (Philippians 2:7–8). The life of Christ involved constant sacrifice for others. He resisted the urge to become a king on a throne and receive "all the kingdoms of the world and their glory" (Matthew 4:8). Even in the last few hours before his death, Jesus washed the feet of his disciples and declared, "Truly, truly I say to you, a servant is not greater than his master, nor is a messenger greater than the one who sent him. If you know these things, blessed are you if you do them" (John 13:16–17).

The antidote lies in becoming the servant of all and considering Christ to be a master whose greatness lies in poor, humble service.

For we are not, like so many, peddlers of God's word,
but as men of sincerity, as commissioned by God,
in the sight of God we speak in Christ.

2 CORINTHIANS 2:17

CHAPTER 6

Great Expectations and the Great Disappointments of Apocalyptic Messages:

Before You Put Your Pets to Sleep, Make Sure It's Really the End of the World

Truly, I say to you, this generation will not pass away
until all these things take place.
MATTHEW 24:34

Behold, I am coming like a thief!
Blessed is the one who stays awake, keeping his garments on,
that he may not go about naked and be seen exposed!
REVELATION 16:15

Then I heard a holy one speaking, and another holy one
said to the one who spoke, "For how long is the vision
concerning the regular burnt offering, the transgression
that makes desolate, and the giving over of the sanctuary
and host to be trampled underfoot?" And he said to me,
"For 2,300 evenings and mornings. Then the sanctuary
shall be restored to its rightful state."
DANIEL 8:13–14

T he end is near!" That's the kind of half-crazed apocalyptic warning you might expect from a disheveled street preacher standing on a soap box and yelling at the top of his voice in any big city in present-day America. You might not have expected it, though, from a shy farmer near the Erie Canal in the mid-nineteenth century. William Miller shocked his community by reluctantly sharing his predictions that Christ would return in 1843—and people listened. (The date would later change to 1844 after a recalculation.) Area newspapers carried stories about the *Millerites*, men and women from various denominations who believed Miller's prophecy and prepared themselves for the coming rapture. Reporters claimed the Millerites dressed in white robes, awaiting this event. Some allegedly stood on rooftops or climbed trees to be the first to go. Other stories surfaced of gatherings in cemeteries, so Millerites could be close to their soon-to-be-resurrected loved ones at Christ's second coming. There were also reports about people giving away their possessions. The Miller-friendly *Signs of the Times,* published by his friend, and local pastor, Joshua Vaughan Himes, regularly championed his views. Atop all of this, the heavens appeared to be shouting apocalyptic warnings. A comet and star showers filled the night skies. The clock was ticking.

In such a situation, you could decide to get in line for the free handouts from people getting ready for heaven, join the crowds of people watching the robed believers (as the papers sensationalized), or get right with God in a hurry.

The Old and New Testaments have several passages referencing this world's end—and the Millerites were not unique in claiming to have special revelations or inspired insights about its unfolding. New York and the surrounding New England area became breeding grounds for leaders who claimed to have insights into when and how the end would come. Central and western New York were particular hot spots of apocalyptic activity. The great revivalist Charles Finney called this area the "burned-over district," based on numerous revivals that had spread like wildfire, exciting an eager crowd that was focused on the return of Christ.

The Latter-day Saints were one such group, following Joseph Smith, who preached about the second coming. He claimed that, between 1823 and 1827, the angel Moroni appeared to him near Palmyra, New York. This angel, according to Smith, gave him God's true gospel during his four trips to a local hill called Mormon Hill, which is perhaps *Cumorah* in Smith's *Book of Mormon* (1830). Smith claimed he translated this book from golden plates obtained from Moroni there. Today, the splendid Hill Cumorah festival is held each summer, drawing nearly forty-thousand attendees. Smith preached that people needed to be ready for the ensuing persecutions. In large part, the group moved incrementally westward. Smith himself was murdered by a mob in Illinois (a story for another day), but his legacy lives on, most prominently in the Utah-based Church of Jesus Christ of Latter-day Saints (LDS).

Ninety-three miles due east from Palmyra, in Oneida, New York, John Humphrey Noyes preached a much different message about the second coming. He claimed it had already happened with the fall of the Jerusalem Temple in AD 70. But Christians would need to show genuine love in a community before God's kingdom on earth would appear. The church, Noyes claimed, had overlooked this part of the end-times prophecy and needed someone like him to help fulfill it. His "perfectionist" colony, first established in Vermont, moved to Oneida in 1848 after Noyes was arrested "on charges of adultery and fornication."[1] The complex socialistic community was based on his theology that one would be free from all sin after salvation. Noyes saw marriage as an extension of perfection and advocated a structured view of free love. In Eden, he argued, there had been no physical shame. Likewise, there would be no marriage in heaven. For now, every man was every woman's husband and vice versa—though relationships were strictly monitored, even controlled. Eventually the perfectionist *free love* doctrine was rejected by the surrounding community. "The spiritual dimension of the utopian community eroded and by 1881 the experiment had folded"—though your silverware drawer might store some Oneida flatware.[2]

Despite his failed end-times prophecy (the world didn't end in 1843 after all), William Miller's legacy has survived, primarily in the Seventh-day Adventist Church. A Miller biography, *Memoirs of William Miller,* published in 1853, notes other millennial groups:

Throughout New England and in the West, Shakers professed that Christ had come spiritually in the person of Ann Lee to establish a new social order. Ralph Waldo Emerson's Transcendentalism attempted through communal societies to perfect human institutions. Universalism, an older movement, complemented or interacted with various millennial and utopian groups.[3]

Against this historical backdrop, *Memoirs* gives an apt summary of Miller's place in history:

Recent scholarship places Miller and those associated with him within the context of antebellum America. Millerites are no longer viewed as fanatics but rather as a part of a dynamic and remarkable period in American history. For Seventh-day Adventists and other religious groups who emerged from the Millerite movement following the 1844 disappointment, Miller is respected as a man of God who brought attention to neglected and important biblical truths and launched a movement that they see as a fulfillment of Bible prophecy.[4]

Apart from his miscast of the world's end in 1843 and 1844, many mainline Christians would find his teachings admirable, just like the estimated eighty ministers in 1833 who signed his license to preach. He found the relevance of the Scriptures for everyday life, believed fervently in the second coming of Christ, and rejected deism's annihilation of the body at death. He knew the latter all too well, since he had been endorsing it for more than a decade before returning to Christianity. Likewise, most people today would likely welcome him based on his time as a War of 1812 veteran, neighbor, and respected community leader. He was a quiet farmer anguishing over what he thought were answers to a question of eternal consequence. Only in the context of his times can we fully understand the traction of his views.

Miller wrestled with Daniel 8:13–14, "Then I heard a holy one speaking, and another holy one. . . . said to me, 'For 2,300 evenings and mornings. Then the sanctuary shall be restored to its rightful state.'" He came to believe the 2,300 *days* mentioned in the passage were actually *calendar years*. Starting in 457 BC with Artaxerxes I's decree for Jews to reenter Jerusalem, he added 2,300 years and arrived at his predicted date of 1843. In AD 1832, Miller began introducing his views to a broader audience by publishing sixteen articles in the *Vermont Telegraph* and, the following year, his first tract: *Evidences from Scripture and History of the Second Coming of Christ, About the Year AD 1843, and of His Personal Reign of One Thousand Years.* Also in 1833, he gave up his justice-of-the-peace duties and turned to full-time preaching.

Accounts of Miller's preaching portray a riveting communicator. Once his words were in print, his relative obscurity was over. The fixed dated of October 22, 1844, became the singular moment associated with what would later be called the "Great Disappointment." Although Miller had originally predicted the Lord's return between March 21, 1843 and March 21, 1844, and one last hope of April 18, 1844, they all passed and he offered a public apology—but sincere belief in Christ's eminent return. However, his predictions took on new life in August of 1844, even though the dates had passed. Samuel S. Snow preached the now infamous camp meeting sermon in Exeter, New Hampshire: "The Seventh Month." Through his re-recalculations of Miller's work using the Karaite Jewish calendar, the exact date was set at October 22, 1844.

Whitny Braun, from a Seventh-day Adventist heritage, addresses the Great Disappointment creatively in a national venue. She is currently an assistant professor of Religion at Loma Linda University (a Seventh-day Adventist health sciences university). She states in *HuffPost*:

> The fact that you are reading this article would indicate that the Second Coming didn't happen. October 22 would go on to be known as "The Great Disappointment", a somewhat unfortunate name as Bill Maher pointed out while talking about Dr. Ben Carson, a member of the Seventh-day Adventist faith, recently. He said of Carson's Adventist beliefs, "Do we really want a guy who is disappointed that the world didn't come to

an end having his finger on the button?" One hundred and seventy-three years later, that interpretation of Scripture is a bit problematic for Adventists. But, on October 22 every year, my Adventist friends and I will jokingly wish each other a Happy Disappointment Day.[5]

Today, the Seventh-day Adventists, a Christian Protestant movement, has more than 20 million members and 81,000 congregations worldwide. William Miller, the passionate, humble successful farmer, likely wouldn't be too disappointed.

New York's burned-over district was certainly not the only source of unique groups espousing special knowledge of the world's end. Let's take a quick tour through history to see other apocalyptic groups in action:

1530s: John (Jan) of Leiden and Münster convinced a group of Anabaptists that the walled city of Münster, Germany, was the New Jerusalem, and that he was the Messiah for that final age. This story is treated in more detail in this book's next chapter, as it represents a significant historical event. Suffice it to say, the iron cages hanging from the nearby steeple are constant reminders of the 1535 bloody end to this heresy.

1666: The Great Fire of London occurred in the most conspicuous of calendar years, containing the biblical number of the Antichrist, 666. This scenario, in the aftermath of the devastating plague, appeared ripe for fruitful speculation.

1874 and 1914: Charles Taze Russell proclaimed Christ would return invisibly in 1874 and then his second coming would follow in 1914. The unfolding of the events and the launch of World War I seemed to give this prophecy a boost—until the world didn't end. Zion's Watch Tower Tract Society and Jehovah's Witnesses grew out of Russell's preaching.

1988, December 31: Hal Lindsey sensationalized the second coming with his best-selling book *The Late Great Planet Earth* (1970), which set forth a 1988 date for Christ's return. When the world didn't end in 1988, he discussed a different possible date, like many other apocalyptic prophets. His latest date, 2000, came and went. In 2009, Lindsey reminded his critics:

> On page 54 of the LGPE [*Late Great Planet Earth*], I wrote, "What generation? Obviously, in context, the generation that would see the signs—chief among them the rebirth of the State of Israel. A generation in the Bible is something like forty years. IF this is a correct deduction, then within forty years or so of 1948, all these things could take place." . . . The verb "know" or "recognize" [the signs of the end times] is also in the imperative mood in the Greek, which means it is a command. . . . I believe the signs I wrote about in the *Late Great Planet Earth* are still valid. In fact, more so now than ever.[6]

1993: David Koresh and the Branch Davidians were thrust into international media with their standoff with federal authorities. Koresh, a self-proclaimed prophet and messiah figure with a martyr complex, took his name after the biblical source of the messianic family line, King David, and Cyrus the Great ("Koresh"), who had freed the Jews. Already with a colorful past, he became their leader after his rival, George Roden, was convicted of murdering another messianic claimant with an axe to the head in 1989. The fifty-one-day standoff resulted in the deaths of Koresh and seventy-nine of his followers in the fires at their Mount Carmel Center—their compound in Waco, Texas, which he claimed was the Davidic kingdom. But these were not the largest casualties of this misguided apocalyptic group. The terrorists responsible for the Oklahoma City bombing on April 19, 1995, timed it on the second anniversary of the Waco destruction. The Davidian group is a distant offshoot from the Millerites, through a splinter of one of the later Adventist groups, the Shepherd's Rod.

1977: William Branham (d. 1965) was a popular faith healer and the pioneer of the movement after World War II. He demonstrated remarkable gifts, drawing crowds of thousands. Branham claimed Elijah had anointed him, providing an inextricable link to his eschatological understanding. He confidently predicted the world would end in 1977. Where did he get this information? From seven angels he claimed met with him in a dark cloud atop Sunset Mountain near Phoenix on February 28, 1963. The angels instructed him to return to his church in Jeffersonville, Indiana, and preach on the seven seals of Revelation. (Skeptics have noted that there is proof that the cloud, pictured in various photographs, is known to be from a failed launch of a Thor rocket near Los Angeles.) Also, Branham said Jesus came to him personally while studying for the sermons, revealing the first seal. His series of seven sermons to his Indiana parishioners would remain central in his huge speaking venues. Branham tragically died in a car crash long before he believed the world would end.

1994 and 2011: Harold Camping (1921–2013), longtime president of Family Radio and a noted Christian broadcaster, made various predictions about the end of the world. This untrained Bible scholar, like many self-proclaimed prophets, claimed to have discovered a secret code in the Bible. When the world did not end in 1994, he noted that he had misread the code. More recently, at age ninety, he predicted the world would end on May 21, 2011. He also compromised on various orthodox teachings, such as his belief in annihilation rather than hell, while also calling Christians to cease evangelizing, because the dispensational door had been shut. Albert Mohler, the ninth president of the Southern Baptist Theological Seminary, was among many theologians and Christian leaders who were livid. Perhaps this frustration was in part because of Camping's massive media platform and/or because of the damage done to the church's reputation and people's theological understanding. "The derision and laughter from the secular community was loud and entirely predictable. An atheist group offered to take care of the pets of those who were raptured, but for a fee."[7] Mohler continues in his rather direct assessment:

> Mr. Camping is not merely wrong on this rather embarrassing matter. More importantly, he has called for Christians to leave their churches, claiming to have found in the Bible the announcement that the age of the church has passed. Since the church no longer exists, he has taught, Christians should leave the so-called churches and merely associate for fellowship. Baptism and the Lord's Supper, commanded by the Lord to be practiced until he comes, are no more, Camping has taught.[8]

End-times predictions aren't reserved only for Bible-based groups and teachers. Consider the bizarre ending for the Heaven's Gate cult, when thirty-nine members committed suicide in 1997. They believed an extraterrestrial spaceship was following Comet Hale-Bopp, and their actions would somehow help them join it. Two years later, many people were worried that civilization as we know it would end in a giant Y2K meltdown on January 1, 2000. In 2012, headlines spread through the media proclaiming a December 12 end based on a controversial reading of the Mayan Calendar that allegedly heralded the end of the Fourth World (the present world) and the final destruction of earth. The list of doomsday predictions goes on and on—and likely will until the Lord really does return.

House of David ball players from "Eden Springs" in Benton Harbor, Michigan.

Shiloh mansion, which was Benjamin Purnell's home. He delivered his sermons from the top balcony beneath the cupola in this image (Benton Harbor, Michigan).

An example of an unsettling Gnostic ritual that induced ecstasy, a transcendental state of mind.

Authorities leading Origen of Alexandria to be tortured for his beliefs. He died after release from his injuries. It is a major irony in Church history; the Emperor essentially killed one of the first prominent Christian theologians for his beliefs, and three centuries later, the Christian Church pronounced Origen a heretic.

Men handling serpents in a worship service.

Prophet Jones, a pivotal leader of the Church of Universal Triumph, Dominion of God, Inc., believed he was the incarnation of Jesus Christ during the premillennial age.

Prophet Jones puts on his trademark $12,900 mink coat—a gift of thanks from two disciples. He modeled his "throne" after King Solomon's.

SIGNS OF THE TIMES

Of the Second Coming of Christ.

J. V. HIMES, EDITOR.]   "THE TIME IS AT HAND."   [DOW & JACKSON, PUBLISHERS

VOL. I.   BOSTON, JUNE 15, 1840.   NO. 6

THE SIGNS OF THE TIMES

Is published on the first and fifteenth of each month, making twenty-four numbers in a volume; to which a title-page and index will be added.

TERMS.

One Dollar a year—always in advance. Persons sending five dollars without expense to the publishers, shall receive six copies; and for ten dollars, thirteen copies to one address. No subscription taken for less than one year.

DIRECTIONS.—All communications designed for the Signs of the Times, should be directed, post paid, to the editor, J. V. HIMES, Boston, Mass. All letters on business should be addressed to the publishers, DOW & JACKSON, No. 14 Devonshire Street, Boston.

Back numbers can be sent to those who subscribe soon.

ILLUSTRATION OF PROPHECY.

"But I will show thee what is noted in the Scripture of truth."

MR. CAMBELL ON THE RETURN OF THE JEWS.

Daniel iv. 9. "O Belteshazzar, master of the magicians, because I know that the spirit of the holy gods is in thee, and no secret troubleth thee, tell me the visions of my dream that I have seen, and the interpretation thereof. Thus were the visions of my head in my bed; I saw, and beheld a tree in the midst of the earth, and the height thereof was great. This is the interpretation, O king, and this is the decree of the Most High, which has come upon my lord the king; That they shall drive thee from men, and thy

signed for the captivity of the Gentile church in mystical Babylon, and will be considered in its proper place.

Literal Babylon fell gradually, just in proportion as the Jewish captives were liberated, but was not utterly destroyed until the last company left, so will this tree, with mystical Babylon at its head, be destroyed, body and branch, stump and roots, just in proportion, and just as soon as the Jews are gathered from their long dispersion, and the Gentile church becomes purified from the harlotry of Rome.

this the author does not assent though the po of resemblance may hold good in some respe

Daniel and Nebuchadnezzar were both t bled at this vision, but it is by no means t supposed that either of them ever understoo deep and extensive meaning. It was desig for ages far future to them. Daniel sat one l in astonishment, and his "thoughts trou him" as the typical interpretation was reve to him. (verse 19.) This had a direct bea upon the person of the Babylonian mona Nebuchadnezzar, for his pride and arroga against God, one year after the vision, was d en from among men, and his dwelling among the beasts of the field, and he was n to eat grass like oxen until seven times, or se literal years passed over him, and until he le ed that the Most High ruled. This, as a ma of history, was fulfilled in seven years, but beautiful allegory, it requires seven prophe times to be fulfilled on a proud and degene people. God warned them repeatedly by Mand the prophets, that if they "would walk c trary unto him," and "would not be refor by him" they should be driven among the be that is the kings of the earth, and be punis seven times for their sins.

This is a long and dreary captivity to Jewish church, the last half of which a degr

TOP: The front page of an 1840s *Signs of the Times*, a monthly magazine produced by Millerites to explain the prophetic interpretations of William Miller.

BOTTOM: After Jan of Leiden crowned himself King of Münster, he turned the capital city into a millenarian Anabaptist theocracy. His Catholic riva executed him in 1536—and hung his bones in a cage on the nearby church steeple. The cage can still be seen today.

S. IRENÆUS.

St. Irenaeus, Bishop of Lyons, was an early church father, known for "Adversus Haereses," which countered the beliefs and teachings of Gnostic groups.

St. Norbert overcomes radical reformer and heretic Tanchelm of Antwerp in the early 12th century.

Nocturnal gathering of robed and hooded Ku Klux Klan men in the early 1920's.

STATUE OF LIBERTY

THE FACE BENEATH THE MASK

RIGHT: Alma Bridwell White, founder of the Pillar of Fire Church first female bishop in the United Sta and supporter of the Ku Klux Klan.

LEFT: An illustration from Alma Bridwell White's, *Heroes of the Fiery Cross* (1928).

TOP: The conquest of Constantinople during the Fourth Crusade.

BOTTOM: Venetians built ships used by Crusaders in the Fourth Crusade.

TOP: The first Australian stamp to feature an aboriginal person, 1950.

BOTTOM: Australian aborigines forced into labor, c1850.

IS THE BIBLE AT FAULT?

The Biblical Outcome

Groups like those we've discussed tend to focus on the Bible's apocalyptic literature, a genre that includes Daniel, Revelation, and portions of Zechariah, along with statements made by Jesus in the Gospels or by Paul in his letters to the Thessalonians. They spend a lot of time and energy trying to decode these often-cryptic texts in order to understand better the timing and nature of the end of the world.

The Millerites focused especially on a passage from Daniel where the prophet encountered "the holy ones" in a vision (see Daniel 8:13–14, quoted above). Daniel mentions 2,300 evenings and mornings in relation to the duration of time that the Temple would be without daily sacrifices. The Millerites interpreted the term *days* in this passage as meaning *years*, so they could apply it to their own situation more than two thousand years later. The number 2,300 was also much less significant than the Millerites claimed. It was likely meant as a symbolic amount that put a finite limit on these prophecies in order to instill a sense of urgency in its listeners and prompt them to take action.

Besides wrongly applying apocalyptic descriptions to contemporary times, some of these so-called prophets were probably drawn to the prestige that comes with having special access to revelation. The democratic appeal of the gospel has a way of leveling the playing field when it comes to accessing God and truth. This can be unsatisfying for those who are interested in status or in being the guardians of some *secret knowledge*. In this sense, many modern doomsday groups had a lot in common with the sectarian Gnosticism that threatened early Christianity. They wanted to elevate themselves above the church, apart from the body of Christ, as VIP members who were in tune with hidden truths that eluded most Christian believers.

Claims for this kind of special revelation usually echoed biblical events such as Moses's meeting with God or his reception of written instructions by an angel in Exodus. Other echoes included claims of Christ's return in the person of another, merely human leader. In each case, cryptic references to dates and places in the Bible were used or manipulated to make these connections and prove the authority of prophecies or leaders who strayed from Christian consensus. By providing detailed interpretations of hard-to-understand and obscure passages, these leaders were able to present themselves as having divine insight and the gift of prophecy, both of which suggest special access to God.

Point of Departure from Biblical Orthodoxy

The point of departure for these doomsday groups actually starts with an orthodox biblical position. A key feature of Christianity has always been the expectation of Christ's return. Christians claim the biblical hope that God will come again soon and that his return will correspond in some way to the end of the world and the inauguration of new heavens and a new earth. This eager anticipation is something orthodox Christianity shares with groups such as the Millerites and the followers of William Branham. The key departure between biblical orthodoxy and these false prophets is in the question of whether the time of the end can be known precisely.

The Bible clearly states the day of Christ's return is unknowable. It's difficult for even novice Bible readers to misunderstand Matthew 24:36, "But concerning that day and hour no one knows, not even the angels of heaven, nor the Son, but the Father only." In this statement,

Jesus is declaring that he is like a groom who goes to the Father's house to build a place to live with the new bride. Until the parents approve of the marriage, the groom continues to work on the house not knowing when the time will come for marriage. In the same way, the return of Christ awaits an unknown time. 1 Thessalonians 5:2 states, "For you yourselves are fully aware that the day of the Lord will come like a thief in the night." If it comes like a thief, the people to whom it comes cannot possibly know the time. With imagery like this, Paul discourages believers from becoming preoccupied with conjecture over the exact date and time of Jesus's second coming. His focus is instead on encouraging a state of readiness and preparation for an unpredictable event.

In one of his parables, Jesus compares his second coming to ten women who are awaiting the groom's arrival. Not knowing when the groom will come, the women must stay prepared with enough oil to light their way in the darkness. In the end, half of the virgins are prepared while the other half are negligent. Those who were prepared are able to make the journey to the wedding when the time comes. Christians are to wait in a similar state of preparation.

Problem Type

Besides contradicting clear biblical teaching that a precise date cannot be known, these groups tend to force the Scriptures to apply a specificity that the texts never intended. The passages in Daniel about the 2,300 evenings and mornings without daily sacrifices were originally a description of the cessation of daily sacrifices under Antiochus Epiphanes. While God could, of course, follow a similar calendar in the future, this isn't guaranteed and there's no way to base this assumption in the text. There's certainly no indication in the book of

Daniel that these prophecies are also intended for groups of modern, North American believers who are reading them halfway around the world more than two thousand years later.

One specific problem we've noted in these kinds of interpretations is the elevation of the whims of the interpreter over and against the intent of the original context. The passages in Daniel were intended to foster faithfulness in the midst of persecution, not to hype the end times or to encourage people to sell their possessions in the hope of rapture. For the Bible's apocalyptic texts, the focus was on encouraging those people who lived in Jerusalem under the reign of abusive leaders. This context is also in view for a book like Revelation, and it goes a long way to explaining why apocalyptic texts speak in coded language about their oppressors. It was a way of hiding their criticism in plain sight. Apocalyptic texts tend to challenge and prophesy the end of existing power structures; speaking in cryptic language was one way of circulating these critiques without censor or backlash from abusive governments or leaders. Ironically, in the hands of certain doomsday evangelists, these coded texts resulted in new power structures and new forms of abuse, precisely *because* of this cryptic language. The sad reality is that pastors and leaders throughout history have exploited the complexity of these texts to gain power and influence for themselves.

ANTIDOTE

The main antidotes against "great disappointments" involve studying the original contexts of the biblical passages and reading them in light of other scriptures whose messages are clearer. The original contexts of books like Daniel and Revelation can reveal not only the original significance of the numbers they use but also principles we can apply as contemporary readers. For example, the emphasis in apocalyptic texts on faithfulness to God in the face of persecution is a principle that will always be relevant. The insights into God's character are also timeless, as God outlasts every imperial power and government and so reigns over all, throughout all time. Just as Christianity survived the Roman emperors' persecutions, Christians today can persevere, awaiting God's power and coming reward. With the more difficult apocalyptic texts, we might start by looking for these kinds of divinely inspired principles rather than trying to simply crack the codes to gain secret knowledge.

It's also good practice to read obscure passages alongside clearer ones on the same subject. For example, it is wise to read elaborate predictions for the end of the world alongside Matthew 24:36, which clearly states we can never know the time or date. This passage should be referenced any time someone claims special knowledge about the end times. Traditional Christianity holds that the biblical texts do not contradict each other and that any claims that contradict what God has spoken previously are lacking in authority. If Jesus is the Word of God who has been present from the beginning, as John 1:1–5 claims, the divine Word has not changed. If the Word of God is truth, then it cannot be self-contradictory. The confusion, then, is not a problem with the Bible; it rests with the interpreter who has claimed special revelation that supersedes the authority of the Word of God.

Then if anyone says to you, "Look, here is the Christ!"
or "There he is!" do not believe it. . . . If they say to you,
"Look, he is in the wilderness," do not go out. If they say,
"Look, he is in the inner rooms," do not believe it.
For as the lightning comes from the east and shines
as far as the west, so will be the coming of the Son of Man.
MATTHEW 24:23–27

For you yourselves are fully aware that the day of the Lord
will come like a thief in the night.
1 THESSALONIANS 5:2

CHAPTER 7

Be Baptized or Be Killed:

Heretics' Bones Hanging from the Belfry

Then I saw thrones, and seated on them were those to whom the authority to judge was committed. Also I saw the souls of those who had been beheaded for the testimony of Jesus and for the word of God, and those who had not worshiped the beast or its image and had not received its mark on their foreheads or their hands. They came to life and reigned with Christ for a thousand years. The rest of the dead did not come to life until the thousand years were ended. This is the first resurrection. Blessed and holy is the one who shares in the first resurrection! Over such the second death has no power, but they will be priests of God and of Christ, and they will reign with him for a thousand years.

REVELATION 20:4–6

And the Word became flesh and dwelt among us, and we have seen his glory, glory as of the only Son from the Father, full of grace and truth.

JOHN 1:14

There is something enchanting about the walled medieval cities often associated in films and literature with chivalry, open markets, and regal venues. But historical sources depict a much darker side of this clandestine era—especially sixteenth-century Münster, Germany. By age 27, Jan of Leiden (or John of Leiden, 1509–1536) had risen to power in Münster through an open election and convinced many that the world was going to perish. He believed only those in the New Jerusalem would survive. Of course, he claimed Münster to be the divinely chosen spot of this new kingdom and that he was the king of Zion. He made these claims during a season of frenzied spiritual activities that included people rolling on the streets during sermons while foaming at their mouths, ecstatic about Christ's imminent return. Lutherans and Catholics became incensed by these teachings—at first appalled at their refusal to baptize infants and then irate at their governance and theocracy actions. As the local Catholic bishop laid siege to the city, many of the Lutherans trapped within Münster's walls escaped. During a time when Catholics and Protestants had much tension between them, they agreed on the need to stop John of Leiden (or, "the Münster Monster").

Europeans were rather familiar with apocalyptic prophecies— and their failures. Melchior Hoffman had endorsed Anabaptist views, traveled throughout Germany baptizing adults, and claimed that Strasbourg was the New Jerusalem where Christ was going to return in 1533. He was preoccupied with the apocalyptic message of Revelation chapter 20, especially the thousand-year reign of Christ on earth. Hoffman saw himself as Enoch, one of the two witnesses assumed to appear in the book of Revelation, who had the task of resurrecting the apostolic church.

Two of his followers, Jan Matthys and the aforementioned Jan of Leiden, endorsed the essence of Hoffman's beliefs but noted his time and place were off. *Christian History* titles its article on this sordid matter, "Reformation's Apocalypticism: Münster's Monster"—but it's not clear if John of Leiden or Jan Matthys is the "monster" in question. By the article's end, both qualify. Matthys shot a city blacksmith for not surrendering his possessions for the common good. Matthys also wanted to execute all "sinners" within the walls (mainly those Catholics and Lutherans who refused adult baptism). Suddenly, so many people were lining up for baptism that the ministers were busy for three straight days. Obbe Philips, a contemporary Anabaptist who rejected violence, said, "He was so violent that even his enemies . . . were terrified of him."[1] The Catholics, Lutherans, and Calvinists outside the walls were all horrified as they concluded that inside the walls children were destined to hell if they died without experiencing baptism. They hoped for an end to this heresy, considering it a cruel theological imposition on the innocent, not to mention the theological ramifications of rebaptizing adults. The Catholic forces prepared to attack the city after trying to starve it into submission (but the leaders seemed to fare better than the rest of the besieged Anabaptists after demanding all goods be shared in common).

Matthys gave a corrective to Hoffman's theories, stating that Münster, not Strasbourg, was the site of the New Jerusalem. He also set an Easter 1534 date for Christ's return. Jesus did not return that day, but Matthys may have met him then nonetheless. He died on that very day when he saw himself as a second Gideon and led a small group outside the walls of the besieged city. According to one account, his genitals were nailed to the city door, his body dismembered, and head displayed on a pike—yet another cruel aspect of the Münster rebellion saga. Robert Wise, writing for *Christian History*, notes that when Matthys died:

Jan van Leyden picked up the mantle, anointed himself king, and began his messianic reign by running naked through Münster in wild religious ecstasy. He appointed twelve men in charge of the affairs of the city, instigating a reign of terror and wild innovations including polygamy. He indulged himself in excesses while subjecting the citizens to austerity. The new millennial kingdom was to be short lived.[2]

It's a wicked story full of "he said–she said" accounts, and most of the sources come from the victors—or the sensible humanitarians, depending on your view. Prince Franz of Waldeck (1491–1553), a Catholic bishop, reflects on these events, "When the city fell into their hands . . . they overthrew all godly and Christian law and justice, all rules of Church, and secular government and policy, and substituted a *bestial manner of life*."[3] This was a rare occasion when Lutherans and Roman Catholics joined forces in the name of religion.

Though many of the accounts indeed appear sensationalized, we know for certain that John of Leiden led a totalitarian communist theocracy for a little over a year. He held absolute power within the confines of the Münster city walls and convinced the masses he was the channel through which God (*theos*) chose to rule (*krateo*); hence, a *theocracy*. His eschatological message reached the Netherlands, forty miles away, and beyond.

Ideas have consequences and bad ideas can bring catastrophe, and so went the fate of Leiden's faithful. His views brought death to Münster citizens via decrees within his kingdom and through a crushing defeat by attackers from outside the walls. The three iron cages hanging from the adjacent St. Lambert's Church (recently refurbished) testify to the very public demise of Leiden and his associates. These cages are visible in a 1607 illustration of Jan of Leiden and the other two leaders (Bernhard Krechting and Bernhard Knipperdolling) facing their executioners. Before he was chained to stakes in the public square, the victors passed Leiden around to dignitaries as a trophy. For over an hour in Münster, the captors tortured the Anabaptists with flesh-ripping tongs before thrusting daggers into their hearts.

In 2014, two rare coins associated with the 1534 rebellion were auctioned off. One coin is from inside the wall, an Anabaptist restruck coin with no images (which were taboo) and inscribed with their core scripture, John 1:14. The other was struck by Bishop von Waldeck after he recaptured the city. He had initially allowed non-Catholics to preach in the Catholic churches—fueling the flames. The records from the Fritz Rudolf Künker auction of the coins summarizes his change of mind:

> It was one thing to tolerate the reformation as long as the churchly propriety and, most of all, the state's power were not affected, [but] an independent commune beyond state control was something that even a politician favorable towards Protestantism could not accept.[4]

The Bishop's coin, valued around $14,000, carries the images of Münster's patron saints, Peter and Paul.

The greater the mind, the greater the chance for error—and Jan of Leiden's giftedness was indeed a tool for his undoing. He converted to Anabaptism in 1533, only two years before his Draconian deeds and three years before his young death. In that time and area, espousing Anabaptist views itself was risky in private let alone such public settings. It was a rather serious matter since *rebaptism* was one of the two "heresies" (along with *anti-Trinitarianism*) that was deserving of the death penalty, according to the Justinian Law Code (AD 529–534). Each local government chose how and when to enforce such decrees, which Zürich, Switzerland, did in 1526. Its famous priest-turned-evangelical-pastor, Ulrich Zwingli (d. 1531), had delivered conflicting messages on the subject of rebaptism. Nonetheless, his messages on the oppressed church gave confidence to those endorsing Anabaptism's merit. Within a few years of the first adult baptisms, authorities tried and executed many of his associates.

Jan of Leiden and most European religious figures would have been intimately familiar with these events. Münster was only around four hundred miles south of Zürich and one hundred and fifty miles from Jan's home of Leiden, Netherlands. Anabaptist sympathizers were pouring into the walled city from all directions, including those with an "apocalyptic stamp" from one of the three main strands of the movement—traced from Melchior Hoffman through Bernhard Rothmann, Menno Simons, and David Joris.[5]

The Protestants themselves had warring factions, especially against those aligning with Anabaptist views like Leiden and his followers. The Anabaptists never preferred their given name, which meant "baptizing again and again," given the stiff legal penalties. The essence of their beliefs was that baptism before the age of accountability is not biblical. Critics considered this not only heresy but horrifying because it could cause children to go to hell if they died before baptism. The Anabaptists willingly and, critics would say, foolishly dammed the innocent to eternal torture. It was reprehensible. In an ironic and sad stretch of Christian history, Anabaptists were often sentenced to death by drowning.

Jan of Leiden's torturous death for maniacal heresy and immorality in 1536 tarnished the image of Anabaptists, especially Mennonites, for centuries. The Mennonites, named after Menno Simons, who had escaped Leiden's megalomaniac rule in Münster, refer to Leiden as "the evil genius of early Anabaptism."[6]

By the time of Leiden's arrival, Münster had become a city of refuge for many of the European "reformers" facing persecution. The rise of the city's guilds had also given unique freedoms outside of the Catholic hierarchy, and they would eventually win the day. The 1525 Peasants' Revolt, though a debacle itself, had fueled interest in a more democratic system and religious openness.

Still in his midtwenties, Leiden was convincing. He enforced his belief that he was indeed the new king of Zion and that Münster was the New Jerusalem. Accounts vary on the purging of "sinners" from the city, allegedly including one of his sixteen wives, whom he beheaded. Karl Kautsky (1854–1938), a German communistic scholar, strongly opposes such stories in his work, and saw Jan of Leiden and the movement more in line with mainline Anabaptists as ones doing what was necessary to survive a siege. Amongst the sensationalized stories of Leiden's failings, the one charge that does stick is the introduction of polygamy, which Kautsky argues was only to bring social stability due to the lack of males through military losses. However logical this might appear, we need to keep in mind the short-term nature of this entire episode.[7]

Also, while giving a plausible dismissal of the few contemporary sources, Kautsky simultaneously appears to be giving an apologetic for socialism; the Münster Anabaptists had an institutionalized communism (out of necessity during the siege). Kautsky notes the main receptivity of sensational Münster sources is by anti-communists. Consider the following exchange in his book:

A recent writer, the anonymous author of Schlaraffia politica, tells us with awe: "Münster became the theatre of the lowest *debauchery* and bloody *butchery* . . . A power was thus established which carried into practice communism and polygamy; a government in which spiritual insolence and fleshly concupiscence, *bloodthirsty barbarism* and *base epicurianism*, were associated with pious renunciation and self-sacrifice. The infamies of which the women of Münster were victims, the Nero-like debaucheries and barbarities of Jan van Leyden and his colleagues, are the historical illustration" of the aim of modern socialism. Nevertheless our writer thinks that in the socialist society of the future "the Saturnalia of Münster will doubtless be surpassed."[8]

What happened behind those walls intrigued and infuriated the world. At a time in history when the Protestants had rebelled against the established Roman Catholic Church, formed after Martin Luther's protests against alleged corruption and scriptural misuse, the warring Lutherans and Catholics found common ground in agreeing on the need to assault the sinful city. The early sixteenth century actions in Münster also show us just how far fallen man can sink in a short period. If Kautsky is correct, even in part, how vengeful and inhumane people can be when they disagree! We also are prompted to ask about how we would settle these conflicts today.

IS THE BIBLE AT FAULT?

The Biblical Outcome

The most overt use of biblical texts involved the printing of John 1:14 on the coins of the Münster economy. This particular scripture was foundational because it mentions the Word becoming flesh so all could see its glory. The Münster leaders aimed to do the same thing by claiming particular verses had "become flesh" for all to see. For example, they used Psalm 2:6–7, which depicts God as having established a king over Zion, and claimed *they* were the divinely appointed rulers referred to in the passage. They used this and other passages to promote their self-proclaimed role in the theocratic system found throughout Scripture.

The kingship at Münster was complemented with the depiction of two unnamed witnesses in Revelation 11 whereby authority for prophesying was granted by the divine King. The proclaimed fulfillment of Revelation also included chapter 20, in which a thousand-year reign of Christ results in the binding of all opponents. The language of a New Jerusalem is taken from Revelation 21:2, where the New Jerusalem descends in the apocalyptic vision of John. This New Jerusalem could be connected with Acts 2:44, in which the disciples relinquished their possessions so everyone could have everything in common—a potential basis for their theocratic form of communism.

Other passages referenced here do not pertain explicitly to the leaders over Münster but to Anabaptists in general. Anabaptists assert that belief must precede baptism and point to texts such as Mark 16:16, Acts 2:38, Acts 8:36, and Acts 16:31–33. These passages describe belief that precedes baptism and, as far they can tell, do not mention children being baptized. This would explain, then, why the commands of the Great Commission in Matthew 28:19 appear in the order they do: first make disciples, then baptize them. They assert this is because discipleship must come before baptism.

Point of Departure from Biblical Orthodoxy

Jan of Leiden's chief point of departure from biblical orthodoxy lies in the assertion that leaders can claim God's authority to fulfill eschatology. Eschatology is the arrival of God's kingdom by God's work. As such, God is the one who brings about the eschaton in the timing and with the leadership he alone chooses. Such an arrival of God's kingdom will not elevate leaders to be dictators. In this way, the leaders at Münster resemble the kings of Israel and Judah who, while claiming divine authority, did not offer justice and righteousness to the community. Rehoboam, (1 Kings 12, 14), Athaliah (2 Kings 11), Ahaz of Judah (2 Kings 16), Omri (1 Kings 16), Jeroboam (1 Kings 11–13), and Ahab of Israel (1 Kings 16–20) are but a few of more than thirty Old Testament examples. Rather than leading people to swear loyalty toward God, the tactics promoted fearful obedience to the leaders of Münster.

Another point of departure can be seen in the claim that God's final kingdom had already come to pass. The efforts to embody Revelation miss the orthodox views that God is the one who will bring about a New Jerusalem after the old heavens and old earth have been removed. Münster, though, is a clear example of how the old heavens and old earth *remain*. When leaders deceive and abuse only to be attacked and executed, the violence against others attests to the *lack* of God's perfect kingdom rather than the *embodiment* of it. The sad fate of many Anabaptists clearly marks a lack of righteousness and justice that God desires. The eschaton has not yet been embodied, and thus none know when God will choose to bring it to pass.

Regarding baptism, the orthodox position is clear and yet unhelpful in the debate that has raged from the early church to the present. The orthodox position is that we should be baptized and baptize others. Whether that chiefly happens in infancy or adulthood does not seem to be as important as it became in the war-torn areas of Europe. Certainly, no orthodox position would condone drowning someone who baptizes adults nor forcing those who were baptized as infants to be rebaptized or be killed. Baptism is a matter of putting to death a harmful way of living; it should not be the cause of even more harm. The clear debate over the legitimacy of infant baptism or adult baptism reveals an effort to fill in gaps that the biblical texts do not address.

Problem Type

The effort to embody Scripture is a noble enterprise as long as the specifics of the Scriptures are not forced to justify actions that benefit some while harming others. To say that God wants injustice to be bound does not authorize binding an enemy that is perceived to be unjust. The leaders at Münster wanted complete authority to rule and thus claimed that authority for themselves. The title of king of Zion is something God must bestow rather than one we bestow on ourselves. Claiming to be a witness like the two in Revelation 11 is rather precarious, too, since those two witnesses die and are resurrected by God—a feature none of the Münster leaders could assert. Identifying a specific town as the New Jerusalem is baseless without key biblical precedents, such as Christ's return with trumpet blasts, a white horse, and seals unleashed. The millennial reign of Christ also comes after the other events in Revelation and requires the physical presence of a scarred Christ. Thus, the main problem type here is the *lack of corroboration.*

The claims to be the millennial kingdom with kings of Zion and witnesses of the New Jerusalem could not be corroborated by the other
features described in Revelation.

Along with lack of corroboration is the problem of *superseding
what is mentioned*. The biblical texts mention a New Jerusalem, not
a new Münster. To replace Jerusalem with Münster is to violate the
texts and try to reposition the location of God's activity. The claim to
be Enoch is similar, because it assumes not only that one of the two
unnamed witnesses is Enoch but also that the leader has replaced
Enoch with his own name. These replacements display attempts
to assert authority that has not been given. If God specifically chooses
Jerusalem, how can someone claim another city as the place God has
chosen? If God chooses a leader, how can someone claim to replace
that leader? Such claims violate the choices God has already made.

The last problem type is that of *dictating what should occur*. Both
the leaders of Münster and their inquisitors claimed authority to dic-
tate who should live and who should die. That right belongs to God.
God alone declares how people should live. A theocracy must be ruled
by God according to God's rules and not the edicts of any one human
leader.

ANTIDOTE

The antidote to the errant claims of Münster's leaders can be found
in Isaiah 5, which contains a song about a vineyard that serves as a
parable for God's kingdom. The vineyard was planted by God with
everything it needed to survive and bear fruit. Rather than bearing
the fruits of justice and righteousness, it produced injustice and un
righteousness. Thus, the owner of the vineyard wipes it away to start

fresh and produce the vineyard of Isaiah 27. This vineyard planted and kept by God would not be isolated from the nations nor act with injustice and unrighteousness. Rather, this vineyard would enable other nations to come to Jerusalem and worship God there. The antidote is God's care for the vineyard and the vineyard's acceptance of its place and role in the divine song.

Another glimpse of the antidote can be seen in Luke 20:9–19. In this parable, Jesus tells of an owner who planted a vineyard and hired tenants to care for it. When the tenants were to relinquish the fruit to the owner, they rebelled and claimed ownership. Such a claim violated their positions as tenants. Despite warnings from prophets and even the owner's son, the tenants claimed the vineyard as their own. However, such tenants would be removed so that the rightful owner of the vineyard could be recognized. Recognizing God as the owner of the vineyard is the antidote to the attempts to seize authority and produce an ideal community.

Regarding fulfillment of eschatological texts, the antidote is restraint. Just as no one knows the day or time of Christ's return, no one can make such a kingdom come. Rather, the prayer must be that *God's* kingdom come and *God's* will be done! No one can force the eschatological events to occur, and any claim that they *have* occurred must be put to the test. We can do this by examining other biblical texts to ensure corroborating events have, in fact, taken place. We must also look for the fruits of justice and righteousness. If those are lacking, we must doubt the validity of the claim. Truly Jesus's words ring true: "Each tree is known by its own fruit" (Luke 6:44).

Regarding baptism, the antidote is also restraint from commenting on what does not appear. The biblical texts do not claim infant baptism is *opposed* to God's work of salvation. Nor do the biblical texts claim infant baptism must be done to *produce* salvation. Rather, baptism displays what God is doing and must come from God. Baptism is not equivalent to salvation; God's salvation is more wholistic and unable to be confined to the act of washing. Instead, baptism fulfills God's purposes of displaying how he can perfectly cleanse what is filthy. The openness of baptism enables it to be an invitation. Rather than forcing others to conform to our ways of viewing baptism, baptism invites us to view God's ways as better than our own.

For false christs and false prophets will arise
and perform great signs and wonders,
so as to lead astray, if possible, even the elect.
MATTHEW 24:24

Pride goes before destruction,
and a haughty spirit before a fall.
PROVERBS 16:18

CHAPTER 8

Early Christian Heresies:

The Ophites and Controversial Alternatives for an Inconvenient Creator

Now the serpent was more crafty than any other beast
of the field that the Lord God had made. He said to the woman,
"Did God actually say, 'You shall not eat of any tree
in the garden'?" And the woman said to the serpent,
"We may eat of the fruit of the trees in the garden, but God said,
'You shall not eat of the fruit of the tree that is in the midst
of the garden, neither shall you touch it, lest you die.'"
But the serpent said to the woman, "You will not surely die.
For God knows that when you eat of it your eyes will be opened,
and you will be like God, knowing good and evil."

GENESIS 3:1–5

Standing by the cross of Jesus were his mother and
his mother's sister, Mary the wife of Clopas, and Mary Magdalene.
When Jesus saw his mother and the disciple whom he loved
standing nearby, he said to his mother, "Woman, behold,
your son!" Then he said to the disciple, "Behold, your mother!"
And from that hour the disciple took her to his own home.

JOHN 19:25–27

Have you ever approached the communion table and seen a serpent slither through the loaves? Me neither. Such a sight would send most of us off screaming, but, believe it or not, that became a common scene during the early church era with the Ophites. The name *Ophite* comes directly from the Greek word for *snake*. They were also known as the *Naaseni*, after the word for *snake* in Hebrew (*nachash*). They taught that the serpent is the hero in the Garden of Eden story. While most Christian traditions view the serpent as seeking the demise of humans, the Ophites saw him as the image of creative wisdom.

About the only thing the Ophites have in common with Jews and Christians is that they all take the Garden of Eden story from the same source, the Bible. Other than that, Ophitism is a different animal, so to speak. This was not the first group to glorify the serpent in the story; the Jews were already aware of heretical groups that were preoccupied with a distorted view of the serpent and Satan. In fact, Jews were using the Ophite label before Christianity began.[1]

Within the first few centuries of Christianity, the Ophites are mentioned in several sources, and some authors, like Philaster, seem to have relied on the much earlier writings of Hippolytus of Rome (AD 170–235). Philaster's *Arrangement* (*Syntagma*), a lost work cited by others, and *Elenchos VI* may actually include a number of groups lumped under the name Ophite, as many strands of the Christian faith seemed fascinated with both an alternate reading of the serpent's role and changing the nature of God. The latter is as heretical as the first. That is, some of these accounts flip the roles in the creation story, actually turning Yahweh, the Demiurge (Creator), into the evil force in Genesis 1–3. They present him as a misanthropic deity from whose rule humans were freed by the serpent. With this reversed view of the biblical text, many of Yahweh's enemies in the Old Testament became the Ophites' heroes. Their overarching theme is the Gnostic notion of resolving the tension between the spiritual realm that the *good* god has bestowed and the material world that the *bad* god has created. They believe the serpent liberated them by giving them the knowledge of good and evil. The Christ of the New Testament, they argue, has a role similar to the serpent's. Although purely spiritual in nature, he worked through the human Jesus to give secret knowledge to the enlightened.

The Nag Hammadi Library, a collection of thirteen books and more than fifty texts found near Nag Hammadi, Egypt (1945), reveals the Gnostic emphasis on the serpent's advice. The snake possessed its insight for that monumental moment, the sources affirm. This insight was supernatural, given by a higher power. This emphasis figures in Gnostic mythology, and many scholars see it as foundational in understanding Gnosticism's rise.

Today's scholars tend to use Sethianism to capture the broader Ophite practices, especially since their surviving text, *The Apocryphon of John (or Secret Book of John)*, is the best extant representation of the Gnostic worldview. Instead of descending from Cain and Abel, these Gnostics considered themselves offspring of Seth, Adam and Eve's third son. Unconvincingly, with no reasonable entailment to the biblical text, they claimed that he was the revealer of knowledge. The Sethians "were generally seen as belonging to the 'Jewish' (or ascetic) branch of Ophitism" or at the least developed on the "fringes of Judaism."[2]

For the Sethians and mainline Gnostics, it wasn't the infinite Creator, Yahweh, who created the universe and earth. Rather, it was an unknowable Primal Father who set things in motion via emanations, beginning with the feminine Barbelo (Thought). Among her emanations was Sophia (Wisdom), who, through a type of illicit cosmic reproductive decision, emanated Yaldabaoth. This deformed offspring is the closest in the Sethians' pantheon to the Creator God of the Old Testament, but it is not much of a likeness. The Gnostic Sethian storyline says Yaldabaoth produced Archons, who then produced Adam. The Archons found Adam to have superior intelligence and hid the Tree of Knowledge to avoid his ascent above them. Eventually, they expelled Adam and Eve for insubordination. Then Yaldabaoth, the deformed Demiurge, seduced Eve and she beget Cain and Abel.

Many of the Gnostic sects had overlapping beliefs, and many proceeded to mirror the Egyptian and Greek myths by developing pantheons and making representations of powers into divine names. The Basilideans were another among many of these sects, named after Basilides of Alexandria (early second century). The sect seems to have resided mainly in Egypt at least through the fourth century, as Jerome refers to them. One of the key sources for this is the late second-century Irenaeus, bishop of Lyon, France.[3] According to the writings of Irenaeus, they taught a series of emanations from an Unbegotten Father of some sort, a common notion among Gnostics. Two of these emanations, or Aeons, were Wisdom (Sophia) and Power (Dynamis) from whom emanated the Abraxas, or 365 descending heavens. Just as Yaldabaoth among the Sethians was several steps below their Primal Father entity, the God of the Hebrews was at the very *bottom* of the list—the ruler over the lowest of all the heavens, earth (which they actually viewed as an illusion).

The Basilideans, who kept many secrets (and apparently forced initiates to five years of silence), had a secret name for Christ, *Caulacau*.

In their view, it wasn't faith that saved one's soul but rather the secret knowledge the person possessed. And, according to Basilides, since Christ was 100 percent spiritual, he couldn't be crucified. Thus, he tricked Simon of Cyrene into taking his place on the cross and then stood nearby amused at his deception. By this common Gnostic notion, called Docetism, Christ only *appeared* to be crucified.

The Simonians are another Gnostic group stemming from Simon Magus, whom Irenaeus labels "the father of all heretics."[4] Known originally for trying to buy spiritual power (simony), he then concocted a fanciful tale of the reincarnated Ennoia, the gods' special feminine "First Thought." A few mishaps with angels that she had created led to Ennoia's imprisonment in women's bodies, including Helen of Troy and a different Helen, a prostitute. Her journey took many forms over a thousand years. Simon offered his adherents a form of salvation through himself and Helen, who is a manifestation of the Holy Spirit.[5]

Various other groups from the first few centuries had their own peculiarities and what we would consider bizarre behaviors. The Marcionites (after Marcion of Sinope, ca. AD 80–150) rejected the Hebrew Bible (Old Testament) because they believed God was too evil to be Jesus's father.[6] They also practiced extreme celibacy, even for those who had already married.

Conversely, the Carpocratians (after Carpocrates) were at the other end of the spectrum. Irenaeus informs us that, because of their belief in reincarnation, they exercised radical and immoral libertine practices to experience everything they possibly could in this life so that they would not need to be reincarnated.[7]

Their *Secret Gospel of Mark* is known through the disputed letter of their harsh critic, Clement of Alexandria (ca. AD 150–215).[8]

According to a controversial passage attributed to Clement, *The Secret Gospel of Mark* includes scandalous material, such as the controversial "naked man and naked man" passage that implies Jesus had sex with initiates. This passage, akin to the raising of Lazarus from the dead in Mark's canonical Gospel, takes place in Bethany and is known only through Clement's letter: "And after six days Jesus told him what to do and in the evening the youth comes to him, wearing a linen cloth over his naked body. And he remained with him that night, for Jesus taught him the mystery of the kingdom of God." Clement strongly condemns the second-century Carpocratians for prostituting the gospel story, written in the mid-60s AD, for their own desires.[9] Like the controversy over the discovery (or forgery) of many ancient texts, this letter, allegedly found by the controversial Morton Smith at the Mar Saba monastery near Jerusalem, has fueled volumes of speculation.

Regardless of how peculiar or bizarre, the common denominator is that these Gnostic sects were heresies, plain and simple. A general definition of *heresy*—from the Greek *hairesis*—in the Christian context is taking a biblical teaching to an unwarranted extreme or bending it to the point of dissent or nonconformity. Using that definition as a guide, it is little wonder that the late-fourth-century bishop, Philaster of Brescia (in Lombardy), put the Ophites among the top three worst heresies (along with the Cainites and Sethites).

The influence of the heresies can be traced through the centuries to beliefs and practices we still see today. For example, the Docetic views among Gnostic groups like the Ophites, Sethians, and Basilideans that Christ had not been crucified dates back to the second century, but it may have influenced the seventh-century

Quran.[10] The following are two English translations of the same Quranic saying, or sūrat. Chapter 4 (*sūrat l–nisāa, The Women*):

> **Sahih International:** And [for] their saying, "Indeed, we have killed the Messiah, Jesus, the son of Mary, the messenger of Allah." And they did not kill him, nor did they crucify him; but [another] was made to resemble him to them. And indeed, those who differ over it are in doubt about it. They have no knowledge of it except the following of assumption. And they did not kill him, for certain. (4:157)

> **Arberry:** And for their saying, "We slew the Messiah, Jesus son of Mary, the Messenger of God"—yet they did not slay him, neither crucified him, only a likeness of that was shown to them. Those who are at variance concerning him surely are in doubt regarding him; they have no knowledge of him, except the following of surmise; and they slew him not of a certainty— no indeed. (4:157)

These Quranic statements suggest the view that Jesus's death by stoning or crucifixion was a misunderstanding. The people had not caused Jesus to die. Such a statement, however, does not imply that the Quran denies Jesus's death completely. On the contrary, Sura Al–Imram 3:55 claims that Allah caused Jesus to die and then exalted Jesus in order to cleanse him from those denying the truth. The Quran also criticizes those who claim to have stoned or crucified Jesus, for it only seemed to them that it had happened—they had not actually killed him. The Docetists argue similarly that Christ only *appeared* to have died but actually did not.

As for the sacred serpent storyline, the church fathers' harsh rejection of Ophitism didn't prohibit it from surfacing its hydra head through the centuries. We even find vestiges of it popping up in twentieth-century Toledo, Ohio in the *Ophite Cultus Satanas*, or "the Cult of Satan." Cleveland's Herbert Arthur Sloane (d. 1975) started the movement, which is sometimes alternately referred to as Our Lady of Endor Coven (after the Witch of En-dor, 1 Samuel 28). These cults bring the ancient Ophite beliefs back to life, once again praising the serpent as the liberator and worthy of veneration.

IS THE BIBLE AT FAULT?

The Biblical Outcome

The Bible fairs differently for each group. Regarding the Ophites, the biblical texts remain unchanged. The Genesis 2 that the Ophites read is the same text that Christians and Jews consider Scripture; the shift comes in the *interpretation* of the story's purpose. The Ophites see in the text a cunning creature who helped the man and woman escape a doomed existence in the material world. The knowledge of good and evil enables humans to embrace the good, spiritual realm and reject the evil, material world. In this way, the good serpent balanced out the evil Yahweh and set the stage for the balance between the *spiritual* Christ and the *physical* Jesus. Without changing the biblical texts, the Ophites have labeled certain characters and aspects as good or bad, thereby taking the text in an entirely different direction.

Groups like the Sethians, Basilideans, Simonians, and Carpocratians kept certain parts of the biblical texts while adding and altering other parts. The notion of God creating everything good was replaced with divine beings who created forces and emanations that could join the pantheon as spiritual beings. By intermingling with humans, these emanations generated pantheons that resemble myths from the Greco-Roman world more than the biblical texts. Accepted biblical passages contributed characters to the narrative, such as Adam, Eve, Cain, Abel, Seth, Simon, and, of course, Jesus. Many of these heretical groups took gospel passages about Jesus even further, using them as launching points for new stories such as Simon taking Jesus's place on the cross or Jesus's interaction with the naked man in the alleged *Secret Mark*. Even Peter's confrontation with Simon was used as a basis for the belief in Simon, along with Helen, as a source of salvation.

Each of the Gnostic groups mentioned recast and relabeled the texts in order to produce a dualistic set of stories. The balance between good and evil served as a constant theme whereby liberation from evil involved a knowledge of what good and evil entails. The teachings of each group provided that knowledge by using the biblical texts how they saw fit.

Point of Departure from Biblical Orthodoxy

We can call Ophitism a bizarre offshoot, a unique twist, or an unorthodox approach. But whatever we call it, it's not Christianity nor is it based on a responsible reading of the Bible—in part or as a whole. Before we go further, note that the early Hebrew and later Greek copies of the Old Testament claim the opposite of these key tenets of Ophitism. References to Satan in the Old or New Testaments do not imply a being worthy of veneration. Christ is not presented as only spiritual or only *appearing* to be crucified. The views of the Gnostics nullify the foundational, orthodox doctrines of the entire New Testament such as incarnation, crucifixion, resurrection, unconditional love, and salvation.[11] Orthodox teaching holds that Jesus actually opposes and defeats Satan.

An underpinning rule of logic here is the law on noncontradiction. That is, two opposing facts cannot both be true at the same time and in the same respect. As we see with other Christian heresies, various teachers and formidable movements were fascinated with repurposing basic biblical texts to support a dualism among the Godhead—a good god and a bad god. This simply isn't in the Bible and isn't *orthodox* or *straight* teaching. Like the serpent theories, it invokes serpentine logic. The orthodox Christian position teaches that God is all-loving, all-powerful, all-good. Thus, Satan only has the power that God allows Satan to have, as we see in Job 1–3.

Regarding secret knowledge, the orthodox Christian position argues that God has revealed himself through both natural and special revelation. The natural revelation is sufficient to encourage awareness of a divine being, and special revelation comes through sources like the Bible and Jesus Christ. These forms of revelation are available to all rather than to a small group who possess secret knowledge. Moreover, the orthodox position is that the biblical texts should not be altered and replaced or, even in part, rejected as the Marcionites urged. Rather, the biblical texts are to be accepted as the means by which we know who God is and who we are supposed to be.

Problem Type

A key problem type is the negation of other biblical texts that contradict the views taken. The elevation of the serpent in Genesis 3:1 does a disservice to the serpent's demotion to crawling on its belly and having its head crushed in Genesis 3:14–15. Even Revelation 20:2 declares the ancient serpent is the devil and Satan, who will be bound and defeated so that the nations would not be misled by him. The accusations of Satan stand in contrast to the passages about the grace of Christ that is made available to all.

The comments about Christ being purely spiritual or not dying contradict the Gospels. John 19:25–27 relays the emotional side of Jesus's humanity as he took care of his mother, Mary. The passage immediately transitions to a representation of his bodily struggle amidst the torture, and it calls Jesus by name several times (vv. 19:28–30), indicating it was Jesus, not Simon of Cyrene, who died on the cross. The passage gives the equivalent of a coroner's report with the piercing of his side:

> After this, Jesus, knowing that all was now finished, said (to fulfill the Scripture), "I thirst." A jar full of sour wine stood there,

so they put a sponge full of the sour wine on a hyssop branch and held it to his mouth. When Jesus had received the sour wine, he said, "It is finished," and he bowed his head and gave up his spirit. . . . But one of the soldiers pierced his side with a spear, and at once there came out blood and water. (John 19:28–30, 34)

The piercing and burial indicate that Jesus was indeed crucified and died. Other passages, like 1 Corinthians 15:3–8, emphasize the importance of Jesus's death along with his resurrection. Regarding Christ being only spiritual, 2 John 7 declares that anyone who denies Jesus Christ as having come in the flesh is a deceiver and an antichrist. These passages need to be considered when the texts in Genesis or the Gospels are being interpreted.

We must also be wary of any claim that ignores or outright contradicts other biblical passages. For example, the claims about the Demiurge and Yaldabaoth's production of Cain and Abel contradict Genesis 4:1–2, where it is explicitly Adam and Eve's union that produces the children. Likewise, the additions that present Simon the magician as a bearer of salvation contradict the words of Peter in Acts 8:20–23, where Simon's attempt to purchase the Holy Spirit reveal his bitterness and iniquity. Even the idea of reincarnation contradicts the biblical claim of Hebrews 9:27 that God appointed us to die *once* and then face judgment.

ANTIDOTE

The antidote for these Gnostic heresies involves careful examination of the Scriptures. To interpret a passage like Genesis 3 as elevating the serpent is to miss the denunciation at the end of the chapter and negative portrayals elsewhere in the biblical texts. This is like the contemporary attempt to cast Judas as the hero of the gospel narrative. John 12:6 clearly indicates that Judas was a thief and John 13:27 declares that Satan entered him to betray Jesus. The opposition against Jesus is opposition against the "image of the invisible God, the first-born of all creation" (Colossians 1:15). Jesus is the hero of the biblical texts from the beginning of Genesis to the end of Revelation.

Another antidote is to avoid inserting into the biblical texts contemporary stories that are fun but fictional. By adding bits and pieces here and there throughout the biblical text, the Gnostics created worlds that were different from what the biblical texts produce. It is not unlike a modern reader trying to force contemporary images into the biblical text, such as portraying the devil as a pointy-tailed, pitchfork-wielding gatekeeper or injecting the image of angels as cute flying babies with harps. These ideas are not connected with the biblical texts and provide very different depictions of the devil and angels. The tendency to fill in gaps like the Simon story or the interaction between Jesus and the naked man in Mark 14:51–52 only distorts the depiction of the characters in the biblical texts.

To avoid the trap of ignoring pertinent biblical texts or adding contradictory stories to Scripture, look at what rabbis, early church leaders, and orthodox theologians say about the passages in question. These commentaries will often take a puzzling text or topic and present complimentary biblical texts to help clarify any points of confusion. Another important preventative measure is to be mindful of other biblical passages on the same topic. John Wesley offers this suggestion in his preface to *Sermons on Several Occasions*, "Is there a doubt concerning the meaning of what I read? Does anything appear dark or intricate? . . . I then search after and consider parallel passages of Scripture, 'comparing spiritual things with spiritual.' I meditate thereon, with all the attention and earnestness of which my mind is capable."[12] The act of comparing one passage with another is a helpful antidote along with the act of meditating on passages in prayer. James 1:5 reminds us that any who lack wisdom can ask God, because it is God who gives wisdom and who does so with generous abundance!

For Christ also suffered once for sins,
the righteous for the unrighteous,
that he might bring us to God, being put to death
in the flesh but made alive in the spirit.
1 PETER 3:18

CHAPTER 9

Corrupted Biblical Teachings:

Tanchelm of Antwerp Marries
a Statue of Virgin Mary

May the God of hope fill you with all joy and peace
in believing, so that by the power of the Holy Spirit
you may abound in hope.

ROMANS 15:13

But you will receive power when the Holy Spirit
has come upon you, and you will be my witnesses
in Jerusalem and in all Judea and Samaria,
and to the end of the earth.

ACTS 1:8

Imagine going to church this week and seeing your pastor bring to the stage a mannequin that looks like Mother Teresa. He even introduces her to the audience as his friend, Teresa. It's not that hard to picture; after all, pastors use props all the time. But let's take it a step further: He marries the mannequin, right there in front of the church. It's not a lighthearted, silly ceremony, either—this is the real thing, an official marriage. You might think you had seen everything, but then picture him passing around an offering plate and asking you to help pay for the wedding (and for his inanimate wife). You might scratch your head and wonder if the pastor is trying to bring the 1987 movie, *Mannequin*, to life. Or if perhaps he has the same fixation on a "RealDoll" as the young delusional man played by Ryan Gosling in 2007's *Lars and the Real Girl*. Shifting from fiction to history, the scene could bring to mind some of the great artists who became obsessed with their mannequin models. After all, this phenomenon launched a genre of art showcased at Cambridge's Fitzwilliam Museum in its 2014 exhibition, *Silent Partners: Artist and Mannequin from Function to Fetish*.

Now imagine a medieval church with a popular priest, properly ordained in a Catholic order, doing something similar. No need to imagine this one; it actually happened! This strange wedding ceremony took place in twelfth-century Antwerp, and the sad thing is that the congregants showered him with offerings. Some of those attendees came "to witness the divinity in him."

Historic sources collected in the *Acta Sanctorum (Acts of the Saints)*, which priests began amassing in the seventeenth century, paint an often-disturbing picture of various church controversies and heresies. Some *Acta Sanctorum* accounts in particular focus on Tanchelm of Antwerp, whom one AD 1124 witness describes as being "able to distribute his bathwater to the fools [his deceived followers], to be drunk as a benediction, as though it were a holy and efficacious sacrament which would assure the salvation of body and soul."[1] The primary sources in *Acta Sanctorum* are invaluable despite how they can often embellish the accounts, especially in accusations about rampant sexual practices that were often lodged against those already declared guilty of heresy.[2]

Tanchelm of Antwerp, the priest-groom of the mannequin marriage account, certainly fit this category of heresy and strange sexual practices.[3] While leading worship, he placed a statue of the Virgin Mary next to him, proceeded with a sermon disconnected from any reasonable reading of Scripture, and then married the statue of Mary. How did he explain this act? This is where it gets confusing. Tanchelm described Mary as the bride of Christ. This flies in the face of reason, one would argue, because Mary was Jesus's *mother*, not his wife. Further, he saw himself as equal to Christ, claiming that the Holy Spirit was as real in him as it had been in Christ. Witnesses of his actions report, "The wretched man became so arrogant in this train of wickedness that he began to say that he was God, arguing that Christ was God because he had the holy spirit, and that he was not inferior, or less like God, since he also had received a plentitude of the holy spirit." [4]

For Tanchelm and many followers, the ceremony revealed that he was imbued with the Holy Spirit, and it was a spiritual union befitting God's chosen. After his wedding ceremony, he put two coffers (or *chests* in some translations) before his congregation and challenged both the men and women to give. This started a giving war between the genders, who each attempted to prove whether men or women were the most committed to God's requests. It was a good day for Tanchelm's financial bottom line, but not for his legacy. The whole affair is reminiscent of Detroit's Prophet Jones and his lengthy pleas for offerings at the Oriole Theater. The primary source recording Tanchelm's marriage is "Letter of the Canons of Utrecht, 1112–1114," and the following is an excerpt of a diatribe lodged against him:

> He ordered an image of St Mary—the mind recoils from re-peating it—to be brought into the middle of the crowd. Then he walked over to it, and joining hands with the image, used it as a proxy in marrying himself to St Mary. He would sacrile-giously give tongue to the usual sacrament and solemn words of marriage, and then say "There, beloved followers. I have married the Blessed Virgin." . . . Sure enough, the deluded people rushed upon him with gifts and offerings. The women showered him with earrings and necklaces, and by this mon-strous sacrilege he made a great deal of money.[5]

However weird or bizarre and certainly unorthodox Tanchelm's heretical views were, he had a convincing hold on a sizeable group of congregants.

Tanchelm even enjoyed political favor at one time, including an appointment to a mission as Robert II of Flanders's agent to Rome to argue for the redistricting of the Utrecht diocese's boundaries. It appears that, after his failure to secure his patron's wishes, his life spi-raled into suspect directions, including imprisonment by the bishop of Cologne. He went from opulent confines to a commoner's lifestyle as an itinerant preacher. His heretical teachings followed these events.

From most accounts he was a riveting speaker and drew crowds. Part of his message was appealing for obvious reasons—he preached the abolishment of tithes! Various examples of this message can be found during the Middle Ages in protest to alleged fiscal abuses in Rome and the papal decrees banishing marriage for priests. These marriage laws created turmoil for many who saw their own spiritual lives and marriages in jeopardy. Tanchelm also preached the banning of the Eucharist and all the sacraments, which undermined the very rationale for a priest's role in the community. The chief job of the priest, after all, was to perform the Eucharist on a weekly basis! If eternal hope was tied to taking communion and only an ordained priest could offer it with God's anointing, then rejecting this central belief and practice would result in catastrophic implications for the Catholic Church.

The expected reaction from local and Vatican officials came, and Tanchelm found himself banned from the churches. One might argue that these were matters of heartfelt beliefs and differences in interpretations, but it went beyond that. Tanchelm's actions and presentation exuded deep arrogance and the pursuit for prestige, which fueled his critics' disdain. He held his services in open fields, which might have seemed rather Spartan, but he didn't let that stop him from making a grand scene. His coterie would march him out in a procession that looked like a cross between the pontificate ceremonies and Caesar's.

The Antwerp letter, after casting him as the "predecessor of Antichrist," captures his open preaching:

> After that [act of seducing women, which may have been a trumped charge that seemed to be added to the heretic's wrongdoings] he moved out of the shadows and bedrooms, and began to preach from the rooftops, giving sermons in the open fields, surrounded by huge crowds. He used to preach as though he were a king summoning his people, as his followers crowded around him carrying swords and flags like royal insignia. The deluded populace listened to him as though he were an angel of God.[6]

In a plea for help, we learn of a "fraternity" of twelve apostles committed to Tanchelm who were carrying on his work. They, too, appeared to have considerable energy and persuasion. "For in truth, our church will come to serious harm if these men are to escape; as the apostle has it, their words crawl like crabs, and destroy the souls of simple people by their blandishments." All of this was because "our Antichrist has disguised himself as a monk."[7]

This raging controversy led to the arrival of St. Norbert, whose campaign against Tanchelm was chronicled in *Acta Sanctorum*. In fact, we know the details of Tanchelm's teaching primarily because of St. Norbert's involvement. Catholics venerate St. Norbert annually on June 6 as the patron saint of childbirth, and he is often symbolized with a unique attribute, the monstrance (a double-beamed cross).[8] Also, a famous fresco captures St. Norbert fighting heretics in the Netherlands (Johannes Zick's fresco in the church of Schussenried Abbey, Germany).[9] He was sent to Antwerp to eradicate the vestiges of Tanchelm's followers in 1124—nearly a decade after Tanchelm's 1115 death.

Tanchelm's teaching and antics may seem silly to modern readers, but we can't assume this would have been an easy matter to handle. Another document in *Acta Sanctorum*, "The Life of St. Norbert," chronicles the heretical uprising and mentions three thousand armed men following Tanchelm around. A common theme in each of the accounts is Tanchelm's amazing speaking abilities, which led some to call him "a heretical preacher of extraordinary subtlety and cunning."[10] Besides these great speaking gifts, it appears he aggressively tried to shift attention more on his appearance than on his questionable beliefs. To ensure people saw him as a shining leader, Tanchelm exuded glitz and glamour. "He dressed in gilded clothes, and glittered because of the gold twisted into his hair, and the many ornaments which he wore."[11] Emphasizing entertainment over worship, his "lavish festivity" seems more reminiscent of the entertainer Liberace than a humble preacher like Billy Graham.

The Middles Ages, like any era, was filled with bizarre individuals with no shortage of self-aggrandizement, like Tanchelm. His hapless end came in the twelfth century, when social conditions and other factors saw "an unbridled cult of saints proliferated."[12] It was also a time when the canonization became the prerogative of the pope.[13] The transition was gradual at best. "Local cults around objects that had no or little relationship with Christianity continued to develop, while the veneration of saints also took forms that, though based on old Christian traditions, evolved in rather unchristian ways."[14]

"Uncharacteristic" is a huge understatement. Many of these beliefs seem just as ridiculous as marrying a mannequin. For example, one thirteenth-century French community bestowed sainthood on a greyhound dog who died saving a child. Dubbing him St. Guinefort, they looked to him as the patron saint of sick children.[15] Or consider St. Ontkommer, portrayed as a bearded woman on a cross, who allegedly gave comfort to the suffering, particularly abused women. According to legend, she was a young woman whose father had arranged her marriage to the king of Sicily. She prayed for God to make her ugly so the king would refuse to marry her. Her prayers resulted in her growing a full beard, which disgusted her father so much that he crucified her.[16] Over and over throughout history, we see examples of people—sometimes with good intentions, sometimes with bad— adding wishful thinking, arrogance, daydreams, and pure imagination to the biblical canon. Through the lens of history, the results are often dumbfounding.

IS BIBLE AT FAULT?

The Biblical Outcome

The use of biblical texts by these medieval leaders is difficult to describe with precision because our sources are mainly critics who sought to demean them as unbiblical. The polemic certainly attacks the actions and beliefs of the leaders, but it is possible to discern some clues regarding how the biblical texts were used. The leaders are not credited with quoting biblical texts precisely but rather using certain themes and features of the texts.

Tanchelm's "marriage" and preaching reveals an attempt to display the power of the Holy Spirit within him. The claim to be Christ seems to have been based on the claim that the Holy Spirit had descended on him in a way that was similar to the descent of the Holy Spirit upon Christ at his baptism. This might even be the explanation for why Tanchelm sought to display his marriage to the Virgin Mary. Luke 1:35 describes the promise that the Holy Spirit would come upon Mary, enabling her to conceive a child. Tanchelm's marriage would enable a union between the Holy Spirit in him and the Holy Spirit in her.

The aim seems to have been to embody Christ in his most glorious moments. Tanchelm's use of gold and glitter might also have been an attempt to embody the texts describing the transfiguration of Jesus, whereby his appearance was changed into a glowing figure. The use of the cross reveals a mystic fascination with how the death of Christ had been glorified. Tanchelm used the cross as an emblem to bring himself glory. The appointment of twelve followers had a similar effect in showing that the leadership of Christ was present in Tanchelm.

Beyond embodying aspects of Christ's life was the attempt to embody the glory of saints and prophets. The veneration of holy people was an attempt to "share in the inheritance of the saints in light" (Colossians 1:12) and, more to the point, to become like that saint. For some, this meant having the miraculous powers that had been ascribed to various saints.

Point of Departure from Biblical Orthodoxy

The departure from biblical orthodoxy involves the rejection of Christological features in favor of what Christ frequently opposed. A good example comes in Tanchelm's proclivity for draping himself in gold and glitter, perhaps to emulate the *light* of God's glory. Given his knowledge of the Bible, it is likely that Tanchelm was aware of Acts 12:21–23, which clearly reflects God's utter disdain for how Herod sat in his magnificent robes after giving a powerful speech. Herod accepted the people's praise that his was "the voice of a god, and not of a man!" Tanchelm desired and accepted similar praise, which would make him more like the Herod who was struck down by God and consumed by worms than like Christ. The glory of Christ lies in the self-sacrifice, whereby he was willing to give up his life and resist the fame from the crowds in order to do God's work. Moreover, the orthodox position is that Christ is the Son of God who alone reigns with the Father and the Spirit forever. Claiming to take Christ's place is to oppose the place that he alone has.

Orthodox Christianity also holds that it was God's power that enabled Mary to conceive and empowered the prophets and apostles to work wonders and heal the sick. Thus, God is the one who works these miracles; they are not superpowers that can be claimed by saints. Even the Greek word for saint has connotations of one who has been sanctified or made holy. A saint cannot sanctify himself. Moreover, the qualification of a saint is holiness, whereby the person is completely dedicated to God like the priests, tabernacle, and Temple items were.[17]

Another key departure from the biblical texts is the denunciation of practices that are encouraged in Scripture. The Eucharist ("Lord's Supper") and baptism are essential components of Christian worship, which some branches of Christianity believe cannot be removed. A denunciation of the sacraments is a denunciation of Christ, the one who instigated them. While not a sacrament, the act of giving tithes to God is a sacred action in both the Old and New Testaments. The tithes were instructed to be given so that the priests and poor could survive. As Paul says in 1 Timothy 5:18, wages are due to the worker, and refusing to provide for the one laboring for the gospel is the equivalent of muzzling the ox while it is treading on the grain.

Problem Type

The problem that unifies Tanchelm and these other medieval figures is an attempt to elevate self in the eyes of the people by appearing to be like Christ or other glorious figures from the biblical texts. The aim of the preaching or statements seems to have been to draw attention to how great the ones delivering the messages were. Tanchelm and heretics like him used divine revelation as a means of pushing their agendas to the crowds, who were expected to accept these messages based on the speaker's charisma. While veneration of saints does not necessarily mean elevating them over Christ, these medieval leaders serve as examples of when such heresy does occur. Leaders like Tanchelm may claim to have authority to speak for God, but their denunciations of tithes and sacraments reveal an opposition to divine revelation already present in the biblical texts.

ANTIDOTE

The antidote for abusing the biblical texts like these medieval leaders can be found in the selfless acts of Christ. He did not claim glory for himself nor consider equality with God something to be grasped. Instead Philippians 2:4–11 declares that Christ emptied himself, becoming a servant and being obedient to death on the cross. Yes, the cross does display glory, but it does so through the act of selfless love that caused Christ as the High Priest to offer himself as the sacrifice according to Hebrews 9:13–14. Regarding tithes, Hebrews 7 declares the appropriateness of Abraham giving tithes to Melchizedek and states that Jesus, a priest in the order of Melchizedek, is therefore worthy to receive the tithes of Abraham's descendants.[18] Tithes are an act of faith that recognize how God has given us all that we have and that he deserves more than we have to offer. Plus, giving tithes provides a small way to curb our greed and self-elevation—the same "you will be like God" temptation the serpent offered mankind in Genesis 3:5. It is this self-elevation that Jesus resisted in the desert when Satan offered him recognition, fame, and power (Matthew 4:1–11). The antidote for venerating ourselves as saints or Christological figures is to faithfully follow Christ in obeying God and humbly serving others.

Do nothing from selfish ambition or conceit,
but in humility count others more significant than yourselves.
Let each of you look not only to his own interests,
but also to the interests of others.

PHILIPPIANS 2:3-4

You shall worship the Lord your God
and him only shall you serve.

MATTHEW 4:10

CHAPTER 10

Under the Hood
of the Ku Klux Klan:

The Problems of Reading
through Errant Eyeholes

And the LORD appointed a great fish to swallow up Jonah.
And Jonah was in the belly of the fish
three days and three nights.

JONAH 1:17

And the LORD went before them by day in a pillar of cloud
to lead them along the way, and by night in a pillar of fire
to give them light, that they might travel by day and by night.
The pillar of cloud by day and the pillar of fire by night
did not depart from before the people.

EXODUS 13:21–22

I've heard thousands of sermons over the years. Most of them were good; many were bad. A few were exceptional. And then there's a special category that you could only describe as total train wrecks. Absolute disasters. These were poorly presented orations, incoherent arguments, and gross misinterpretations of the biblical text. None of the disasters I've sat through, though, could compare to some of the abhorrent sermons coming out of Indianapolis in the early 1920s. There, in a lovely Victorian building in a nice neighborhood, crowds of a thousand or more would file in every week. If you were there, you'd notice that all the participants were white. The men wore neatly pressed shirts and near-matching suits; the women chatted in groups and attended to the children. It would no doubt look like a scene taken straight out of a Norman Rockwell painting. But then, the sermon would start and you'd realize something had gone horribly wrong.

Jonah 1:17 was a commonly preached passage at the time among some pastors. Maybe you've heard trite sermons about the wayward prophet Jonah and God's miraculous intervention to keep the missionary on course. That's not what you would hear in *this* church. Instead, the pastor would begin unpacking the *real* meaning of Jonah and the whale: instead of Jonah protesting the Assyrians in Nineveh, the preacher would contend with intense emotion, the real point is that the Jew was so foul in the whale's mouth that even a fish couldn't stomach him. *That's* why the whale spat him out. Semites, according to this fellow, make even fish vomit.

This kind of hateful rhetoric seems unthinkable in the American church today, but at that time, in that place, and among those crowds, it struck a nerve—and the message of bigotry spread from pulpits for years to come. I'm talking about the heyday of the Ku Klux Klan.

The near east side of Indianapolis is home to various buildings connected to Ku Klux Klan (KKK) history. Englewood Christian

Church, though prominent today for its widespread (and evangelical) ministries to the disenfranchised, did indeed kick out one of its ministers, the Rev. F. E. Davison, in a Klan-related scandal. His offense: *refusing* to allow the KKK to meet there! Davison chronicles the whole affair in his 1955 book, *Thru the Rear-View Mirror.* The Klan wanted to make sure that Protestants kept a stronghold against the surge of Catholics moving into the area. One of the many cartoons in KKK publications by evangelical preacher, Branford Clarke, shows the Pope trying to hide behind a sign, "I am a Church."[1] Another of Clarke's cartoons depicts a Klansman swinging a club with the word "BALLOT" and a monstrous, hairy arm marked "ROME" grabbing American soil.[2] Anti-Catholic sentiment was high, especially in Indianapolis due to the influx of European immigrants.

Political, pastoral, and publishing support of the Klan spiked in the 1920s, with the *Fiery Cross* as its new magazine. Indianapolis was no exception. The *Fiery Cross* was actually printed in downtown Indianapolis, only 2.3 miles west of Englewood Church.

Early in the same decade, the KKK Grand Dragon, David C. Stephenson, purchased the prominent mansion on 5432 University Avenue, known today as the Graham-Stephenson House.[3] Although the 1920s were the height of the Klan's power in Indiana, boasting 250,000 members, his time in the mansion and in control was short-lived. His abduction, rape, and murder of a state education staff member led to his imprisonment in 1925, and he spent the next two decades behind bars. The mixed message of Christian beliefs and Klan doctrine remains in stone in the USVA Mountain Home National Cemetery in Johnson City, Tennessee, as the prominent feature on Stephenson's grave marker is an engraved cross. Stephenson's name inexplicably remains on the Victorian mansion.

Today, some of these same near-east-side-facilities once frequented by Klansmen and Klanswomen are overseen by the orthodox and socially active Englewood Christian Church members. The congregation is the progenitor of the up-and-coming mainline evangelical *Englewood Review,* which is beginning to have national reach for those wanting informed book reviews. However, unlike the musings of KKK artist and pastor Branford Clarke, this is a solidly orthodox enterprise with traditional support for the Nicene Creed and a conservative view of Scripture. Ironically, two major Catholic institutions are a block away from this same church. And coincidentally, Graham-Stephenson mansion, like the *Fiery Cross* publishing house, is only 2.3 miles away, but due east instead of due west. The Englewood Christian Church website reflects on the mid-twentieth-century realities:

> Throughout her years, Englewood has taken on the form of either her religious environment or her cultural environment. Until the late fifties, the church looked in form like any other church in Indianapolis with certain "Christian Church" differences, and people held the same views as most of their neighbors. This would explain how some could be Englewood church members, Masonic lodge members and Ku Klux Klan members simultaneously.[4]

While buildings and appearances often tell one part of a group's history, let's turn to the real underpinning of that bizarre interpretation of Jonah, which is among the KKK's officially sanctioned teaching materials. The two main resources we consider here are by Bishop Alma Bridwell White (the first female bishop in the United States) and the Imperial Wizard (international leader) of the KKK, ironically named Hiram Wesley Evans. His strong letter of endorsement is in the front of White's *Heroes of the Fiery Cross.* He states, "I have no hesitancy in commending your book in the very highest terms."[5] Evans's endorsement, along with his countless other statements, rallies, and publications, provide an overt link between the KKK and an official recognized in a church hierarchy. The steady stream of KKK cartoons from Pastor Clarke accents these connections. The Imperial Wizard's view of this is unmistakable. In the same letter, dated November 11, 1927 and addressed to "My dear Bishop," he states:

> The more I see of the work you are doing, the more I am impressed with the magnitude of the results obtained for the common cause for which all Christian Americans are so vitally interested. I hope that Almighty God, in the plentitude of His power, will spare you many many years to continue your work and that this is but the fore-runner of many books which will leave their imprint on our times.[6]

Bishop White was the founder of the storied Pillar of Fire Church, which began in Denver, Colorado (1901) and exists today as Pillar of Fire International in New Jersey. An offshoot of Methodism, it grew to around fifty sites during the KKK's renaissance. Today, it has fewer than ten. After parting from Methodism, it claimed Wesleyan affiliation; its founding beliefs, however, and those through much of the nineteenth century, were antithetical to core Wesleyan teachings—or *any* orthodox teaching, for that matter. The flagship Wesleyan university associated with The Wesleyan Church, Indiana Wesleyan University (IWU), is just up Interstate 69, an hour from the Englewood Christian Church and the Graham-Stephenson mansion. The school of religion at IWU is actually housed on the very spot where the Underground Railroad ran through the campus.[7] The Wesleyan Church (then Wesleyan-Methodist) parted ways with mainline Methodism, but unlike Bishop White and her movement, the Wesleyans split over the issue of slavery. Wesleyans were ardent abolitionists—the exact opposite position Bishop White and the Pillar of Fire Church espoused at that time.

Much is made of the KKK attire, the white sheets with eyeholes, and their appearance in night lynchings. There were many distinctives to Klan customs and attire, but, for now, let's lift up those sheets and pull a beliefs manual from their pockets—one of Bishop White's own books, endorsed by the Imperial Wizard himself. This analogy of peeking under their hoods directly reflects the first major cartoon in Bishop White's *Heroes of the Fiery Cross.* It is a Clarke illustration of the Statue of Liberty holding a Bible, lifting up a Klansman hood as if she just revealed her identity, with the caption, "The Face Beneath the Mask."[8]

Bishop White gives her illogical rendering of Matthew 15:13–14, noting that these verses capture Jesus's response to Pharisees who were offended by his teachings. The passage reads: "He answered, 'Every plant that my heavenly Father has not planted will be rooted up. Let them alone; they are blind guides. And if the blind lead the blind, both will fall into a pit.'" White responds, "The Klan is a tree of God's own planting and it will never be rooted up until it has accomplished its work. . . . Those who criticize this organization and find so much fault with its methods are blind, and if they do not repent and make amends they will fall into the ditch they have dug for others."[9] Her advice on James 3 is equally defensive, especially her take on verse 8, which says, "No human being can tame the tongue. It is a restless evil, full of deadly poison." She concludes, "How much people will have to account for who have criticized, and in their hearts have cursed the Klan, God only knows."[10] She later likens Catholics to blind moles, needing the knights of the Ku Klux Klan to "assume the leadership and be the eyes for the blind [Catholics] during this time of peril. They must name candidates who can be safely trusted." Trusted with what? She continues, "Questions of such vital importance . . . [like] white supremacy."[11] Keep in mind, this is one of the key playbooks of the KKK.

One of the more bizarre interpretations of a scriptural passage is Bishop White's take on Job and the loss of his property. She begins with an ample description of Satan testing Job by taking his servants and property. Then, she makes the leap to American slave owners, "Not all slave owners had the strength of character that Job had when he proved his integrity and loyalty to God during his time of testing."[12] In her opinion, the abolitionists just didn't understand this and other dynamics:

> A strong attachment as a rule existed between the negro servants and their masters which could not easily be broken. When it came to taking away a colored "Mammy" from the children she had brought up for her white master, even nursing them at her own breast in an extremity, there was more involved than a Northerner could readily comprehend. This aspect of slavery was never taken into serious consideration by hot-headed Abolitionists . . . Harriett Beecher Stowe, in her book, *Uncle Tom's Cabin,* brought out this feature which touched the hearts of the slave-owners as well as of others. . . . and was truly inspired of the Lord.[13]

Bishop White's manual for multitudes of Klansmen and Klanswomen turns *Uncle Tom's Cabin* into a manifesto for faux plantation humanitarianism—it "moved to tears" every Southerner and

"Mrs. Stowe proved to be a friend to the South."[14] It was, she contends, the Northerners "who had no particular love for or interest in the colored people."[15]

In the event that you think this might be misrepresenting Bishop White and the popular manual of the KKK, let us look at her blatant statements about the sons of Noah and the Tower of Babel. She explains:

> Noah awoke from his wine and said, "Cursed be Canaan [Ham]; a servant of servants shall he be unto his brethren." "Blessed the Lord God of Shem; and Canaan shall be his servant." "God shall enlarge Japeth [the white race], and he shall dwell in the tents of Shem; and Canaan shall be his servant" (Gen. 9:25–27). This edict was imposed by a wise and just God, and should not work a hardship on the black race. It cannot be otherwise than it should be for their good. Until the curse is lifted from the human race, the very best position that the sons of Ham could be placed in is that of servants [not slaves], thus establishing white supremacy as foretold more than four thousand years ago.[16]

Perhaps no other passage among KKK literature underpins the atrocities done in the name of the Bible (or Christianity) more than this one. Regarding interracial marriages, she sees it as gross negligence and weakness for a *superior* race to take advantage of an *inferior* one for sexual gratification. With the Tower of Babel as her proof text, she contends that God cursed the builders for the express purpose of stopping interracial marriages. She argues, "The only hope of civilization is to preserve unmixed the blood of the races."[17] So serious is this interpretation that she invokes the curse of the plagues in Revelation 22:19—"God will take away [the offender's] share in the tree of life and in the holy city"—if anyone should disagree with her.

Furthermore, Bishop White somehow takes Pontius Pilate and King Herod's involvement in Christ's crucifixion as a parallel of the tandem forces of Roman Catholicism and Judaism against Christianity. "The Jews are as unrelenting now as they were two thousand years ago. Imperial Romanism has never changed, whether represented by the Caesars or the Triple Crown. World domination has always been its goal."[18] Thus, Protestant superiority was somehow given a biblical underpinning, proof texting it with cases like Charles Lindbergh and the "Spirit of St. Louis." She notes the failure of two French Catholic pilots predating his successful attempt and then boasts, "It remained for an American [Lindbergh] . . . to show that Protestantism is to set the standard of the world."[19] She was likely aware that Lindbergh was a staunch isolationist, widely condemned as anti-Semitic for harshly criticizing Jewish newspapers, and adamantly opposed to war even in the face of the Jewish pogrom in Europe. President Franklin Roosevelt banned him from serving in the military, even after the attack on Pearl Harbor.

On this theme, Bishop White comments on Hebrews 12:14, which reads, "Strive for peace with everyone, and for the holiness without which no one will see the Lord." She responds, ". . . but there is such a thing as crying 'Peace, peace!' when there is no peace."[20] She continues:

There is too much passive indifference on the part of Protestants today when the knife is at the throat of liberty. Another world war in this generation can be prevented if Protestants will do their duty and live up to the principles on which the nation was founded.[21]

We know from the infamous "Mississippi Burning" trials of 1967 and 2005 that the link between the Klan's official teaching documents and its members' horrific actions was central to the guilty verdict. Sam Bowers, the Imperial Wizard of the White Knights of the Ku Klux Klan of Mississippi, ordered the 1964 attack ("Plan 4" of his master plan) on civil rights activist Michael Schwerner, whom the Klan called by derogatory names because of his Jewish heritage. During the trial, a Klansman shared that Bowers bragged, "It was the first time that Christians had planned and carried out the execution of a Jew."[22] This single statement, as much as any other in modern American history, echoes through this book's subtitle, *How the Bible Has Been Misused to Justify Evil, Suffering, and Bizarre Behavior.*

The Klan's anti-Semitic posture, errantly tied to the story of Jonah, is manifest in their racist murders. Much of the world saw this on full display as details surfaced of their morbid burial of Michael Schwerner, Andrew Goodman, and James Chaney in Mississippi in 1964. Even tons of dirt at a remote earthen dam on Olen Burrage's farm couldn't bury the ways the Bible was used to justify eliminating opponents. Burrage had bragged to Klansmen about dealing with visiting civil rights workers in 1964: "I've got a dam that will hold a hundred of them."[23] The case wasn't officially closed until 2016, long after the bodies had been exhumed and duly buried.

Official KKK texts allege that the Jonah story, as stated in the Bible, is "clearly" about the Jew being the stubborn nemesis of Gentiles. That is, that "though few in number the Jews remain as much intact and as subservient to the old regime as they were when they rejected and

151

crucified their Messiah." Except for Job, they contend, Jonah's story is the "least understood" out of the entire Bible. The Jew, the KKK maintains, is "indigestible, inflexible, and unbreakable as was proved in the case of Jonah in the stomach of the great fish." In other words, only the KKK gets it right, according to them, noting that even a fish can't stomach Semites.[24]

The KKK often argued that the Bible should be taught in the public schools. Bishop White cites Psalm 119:11, 104, and 105—passages that demonstrate the value of and need for a right understanding of God's Word—and devotes an entire chapter to this in *Heroes of the Fiery Cross*. The first page of that chapter, however, reveals the author's true intentions by blaming the Bible's removal from public schools on some Jewish-Catholic conspiracy. Later, she shifts to modern notions and contends, "There is no better way to offset destructive influences than by the study of the Scriptures. The Bible will stand on its own merits."[25] A full-page Clarke cartoon is on the opposite page from these statements, and it's of a Klansman in a rescue boat racing through the water. On its side is written "THE BIBLE IN THE PUBLIC SCHOOLS." The illustration's caption reads, "The lifeboat to the rescue."

IS THE BIBLE AT FAULT?

The Biblical Outcome

The Klan didn't get much right in its interpretation of the Bible—or in anything else for that matter—but we can say it was at least consistent in the way it warped and manipulated biblical passages to serve its agenda. It used peaceful and redemptive narratives to criticize and subjugate its opponents, a class of people that included everyone from Roman Catholics to immigrant minorities, focusing especially on African Americans and Jewish people. The KKK's approach to this last group provides some of their strangest interpretations.

The Bible is full of passages where God's people, Jews and Gentiles, make mistakes and fail in God's hopes for them. Stories of this type that seem critical of Jewish characters, like the story of Jonah, are highlighted and presented as indictments of the Jewish people as a whole. In their reading, Jonah becomes paradigmatic for all Jews for disobeying God, and the presence of a Jew, intolerable for the Klan, is reinterpreted as inducing nausea and repulsion even to a fish. The same can be said for the chief priests and Pharisees who called for the crucifixion of Jesus. A key text used by the KKK in this regard is Matthew 27:25, in which the people declared the blood of Jesus should "be on us and on our children." This blame of the Jews for the death of Jesus was often coupled with passages like John 7:13 and Acts 17:13 to argue that the Jews consistently opposed Christ and his followers.

The Klan's biblical critique of Roman Catholicism is equally absurd. New Testament passages critical of Roman citizens and representatives were used to criticize the "Roman" church. The actions of Pontius Pilate and the Roman guards who beat and crucified Jesus were identified with the Roman church, which was supposed to share the blame for having participated in Jesus's execution. Moreover, the treatment of Paul and the oppression of John at the hands of the Romans were also offered as indictments of this *foreign church* on American soil; it was "un-American."[26] Apocalyptic texts like those in Daniel and Revelation were applied to Catholicism in a way that identified it with the fallen Babylon or Revelation 18, "the habitation of devils (KJV)" and a litany of other sordid descriptions.[27]

As we know, African Americans were not spared this bizarre interpretation. A number of passages were misused in order to abuse and discriminate against this people group. The curse of Ham in Genesis 9:20–27 is notorious in this regard. In the days of the transatlantic slave trade, Noah's statement that Canaan shall be a slave to his brothers was applied to kidnapped and trafficked Africans who were forced into servitude. The African race was said to be descendant of Canaan and thereby sentenced to perpetual slavery. And, of course, Paul's comments in Ephesians 6:5—in which he instructs slaves to obey their earthly masters—were viewed as explicit and unilateral support for slavery and the ownership of human beings.

The biblical and Christian symbol, the cross, was also abused in the harassment of the Klan's enemies. Just as the medieval Scots set fire to hillside crosses to instigate battles, the KKK first started lighting crosses in Georgia on Thanksgiving Day in 1915. The act was a declaration of faith that any opponent of the KKK (and so of Christ) would see the *light* of what happens to God's opponents: they would burn, like the lake of fire in Revelation 20:9–10. Even the white robes that Klansmen wore as they persecuted others can be connected with the white robes of martyrs in Revelation 7:9. Sadly, we could fill page after page with strange Klan readings without exhausting this group's peculiar perversion of the gospel.

Point of Departure from Biblical Orthodoxy

Right off the top, we can say that the central departure for Klan inter-pretation is the use of biblical texts to subjugate others in hatred. We all know that "God is love" (1 John 4:16) and that, "If anyone says, 'I love God,' and hates his brother, he is a liar" (1 John 4:20), but the Klan is apparently still unaware of this. The prominence of love and compassion throughout many other biblical texts is equally difficult to miss. Additionally, the Bible repeatedly insists that hatred of others is unacceptable to God. Jesus says in Matthew 5:22 that anyone who is angry with another is liable to judgment, and, in doing so, he echoes the command in Leviticus 19:18 to love one's neighbor as oneself. These *neighbors* include those who are racially, theologically, economically, and politically different than we are, just as we see with the Samaritan in Luke 10:25–37. Moving on from one's neighbor, Jesus goes even further to urge in Matthew 5:43–48 that we should love even our enemies. Rather than subjugating opponents, Christianity endorses praying for them and demonstrating the love that Christ showed in dying for those who are still sinners. In this way, love is the fulfillment of the law and the embodiment of the Scriptures. As John concludes, "Anyone who does not love does not know God, because God is love." (1 John 4:8).

Another passage that gives the Klan trouble is Revelation 7:9, which indicates the faithful followers of Christ come from every nation, tribe, people, and language. In this vision, it is not an angry group of white North Americans who are wearing the white robes; it's the universal church, multicultural and multiethnic. The church the Bible promotes is diverse and open to any who believe in Christ and seek to follow him.

The most obvious issue with Klan interpretation is that Jesus was

Jewish. To oppose all Jews is to oppose Christ. Moreover, Jesus's ancestors include a descendant of Canaan named Rahab and a descendant of Moab named Ruth (Matthew 1:5). This illustrates that intermarriages among racially diverse couples are in line with biblical orthodoxy. Moses's marriage to a Cushite woman is a good example of this endorsement, as Aaron and Miriam's criticism of this union provokes divine punishment (Numbers 12:1–16). The union of Ruth and Boaz is another example of divinely sanctioned and favored interracial marriage (Ruth 4:13–21).

Of course, Paul was both Jewish *and* Roman, so logic demands he'd be an enemy of the Klan on two counts. These kinds of issues make it clear this group can't produce a serious study of the Bible without cannibalizing its own sacred text.

Problem Type

We might say that the Klan's biggest problem with interpreting the Bible is its apparent inability to actually *read* it. Some of its exegesis would fail primary school standards for reading comprehension. The driving undercurrents of the text, like so many of its central themes, are ignored as this group chooses instead to superimpose its own meanings on selected texts that are cherry-picked for their usefulness to its purposes. This approach of taking passages out of context and overlooking others is a purely utilitarian reading of the Bible, and Bishop White is a master of this approach. She traffics in a twisted brand of proof texting, where passages are isolated and used for arguments that don't appear in the text itself. Even relatively harmless proof texting by less-biased interpreters than White has the potential to reduce the Bible to a tool for debate rather than a source of truth.

One important corollary of proof texting is the tendency to develop a canon within a canon. Favored verses, those most useful for our arguments, tend to receive a disproportionate amount of attention while other passages, or entire books or testaments, are ignored. Naturally, the biblical texts preferred by KKK leaders are those that present their opponents in a negative light. Passages about loving neighbors and enemies, or offering the gospel to all Jews and Gentiles, are, on the other hand, neglected. Passages like John 7:13, where the Jews are described as opposing Jesus, are acknowledged. Passages like John 8:31, which mentions a number of Jews who *did* believe Jesus, are ignored. This tendency to pick and choose the parts of the Bible we want to acknowledge is a temptation for all of us. Groups like the KKK provide helpful examples of how bad and distorted things can get when we develop canons within the canon to support our personal views or agendas.

ANTIDOTE

The most important antidote to these problems is to be sure that every interpretation foregrounds the biblical priority of love. Another antidote is simply listening to those who are different from us. Those targeted by the Klan had valid criticisms of this group's isolationist principles and they each had something to teach this group about the Bible and the way we should read it. By refusing to listen to those other voices and instead obstinately pressing on with terrible biblical errors, the KKK demonstrated the type of blindness Jesus condemns in Matthew 7:3, "Why do you see the speck that is in your brother's eye, but do not notice the log that is in your own eye?" As we read the Bible, we should not be arming ourselves with verses for argument, but rather searching our hearts for those ways in which we are opposing the perfect Word of God.

———————————————————

And what you have heard from me in the presence
of many witnesses entrust to faithful men,
who will be able to teach others also.
2 TIMOTHY 2:2

For the weapons of our warfare are not of the flesh
but have divine power to destroy strongholds.
We destroy arguments and every lofty opinion
raised against the knowledge of God,
and take every thought captive to obey Christ,
being ready to punish every disobedience,
when your obedience is complete.
2 CORINTHIANS 10:4–6

CHAPTER 11

When the Crusades Became the Killing Fields:

The Ramifications of Misplaced Doctrinal Beliefs

"Yet even now," declares the LORD, "return to me
with all your heart, with fasting, with weeping,
and with mourning; and rend your hearts
and not your garments." Return to the LORD your God,
for he is gracious and merciful, slow to anger,
and abounding in steadfast love; and he relents over disaster.

JOEL 2:12–13

You prepare a table before me in the presence
of my enemies; you anoint my head with oil; my cup overflows.
Surely goodness and mercy shall follow me all the days
of my life, and I shall dwell in the house of the LORD forever.

PSALM 23:5–6

Constantinople was one of the thirteenth century's most impregnable cities—until the world turned upside down in 1204 when it fell to other Christians. The city's walls were about to crumble under the coming onslaught of the Fourth Crusade (1202–1204), also known as the *Christian Crusade*. And it was anything *but* Christian.[1]

The Fourth Crusade proved miserable, as well; at least two popes eventually apologized for what happened during that dark period. The strongest medieval pope, Pope Innocent III, had called for the Crusade in 1198, commissioning the popular Fulk of Neuilly to preach. Unlike the Third Crusade led by Emperor Frederick I Barbarossa, the Fourth Crusade did not just pass through Byzantium under Greek Orthodox control; it turned against its Christian counterparts. It was an ominous sign that Alexius (later Alexius IV) approached the Crusade leaders to restore his deposed father as eastern emperor. Alexius's uncle and usurper Alexius III had deposed, imprisoned, and blinded his father, the Byzantine Emperor Isaac II. Between that political request for vindication and financial woes of the crusaders, the Fourth Crusade became a complex mess.

Constantinople had royal clout and military supremacy, and it had withstood various sieges since its founding nearly nine hundred years earlier. In a very real sense, if you were a Constantinople resident in 1204, you would have been at the center of the civilized world. The city (modern Istanbul) is strategically situated on the divide between Europe and Asia and joins the Mediterranean and Black Seas. Named after the fourth century's Emperor Constantine the Great, Constantinople's very name exudes power. Its massive Theodosian Walls link its legendary defenses to another emperor, Theodosius II, who built the massive fortifications well beyond the former walls, thereby extending the city. The city's inhabitants would have felt more secure than any other people group during the turbulent Middle Ages.

Then the unthinkable happened. The city was demolished, but it was neither Muslims nor pagans that finally sacked the city; the invaders were Christians from France and Venice! Catholic Christians, aided by Venetians, invaded while claiming the blessing of Pope Innocent III. They were *crusaders* under the same cross that most in Constantinople revered and served the same Christ they worshipped. Over four thousand knights and around fifty thousand foot soldiers surrounded and breached the walls. Instead of a grand reunion with a massive force of Christians headed to the Holy Lands, it was war. This attack came after the Catholic crusaders and Venetians pillaged the city of Zara—a Catholic city no less!

They had all come with sworn spiritual allegiance to the message of the cross at the Pope's bidding. Although Innocent III instructed the crusaders not to attack fellow Christians, the Crusades' leaders withheld his decrees from the pilgrims. Imagine the confusion, then, especially for the Catholic Christians in Zara (in the southwestern part of modern Croatia, the former capital of Dalmatia). The leaders of Zara had orchestrated a peaceful surrender, and even this was rejected by the greedy Venetians and an important contingent of the French crusaders. The French owed the Venetians an inordinate amount of money for their transportation, mainly because only a fraction of their soldiers had shown up in Venice. Each crusader was to pay his own way, so when over half of those expected to go to Venice had found alternate transportation, only eleven thousand, instead of thirty-five thousand, arrived in Venice. The Venetians had made a significant investment in the deal, and now the smaller group of Crusaders couldn't pay the full amount owed to them for shipping.[2]

An eyewitness to this hypocrisy was Niketas Choniates (Akominatos), who wrote his *History* shortly after the event (1118–1207). He was a government official in Constantinople who writes:

In truth, they were exposed as frauds. Seeking to avenge the Holy Sepulcher, they raged openly against Christ and sinned by overturning the Cross with the cross they bore on their backs, not even shuddering to trample on it for the sake of a little gold and silver.[3]

Zara's Christians had even displayed Catholic banners from their windows, reminding the pilgrims of their common bond not only in Christ but via Rome. The crusaders supposedly were on their way to free Jerusalem from Saladin and the Muslims. These crusaders were Christians who fought under the banner of the cross and even with the cross affixed to their garments (Latin pl: *crucesignati*) because they had taken a vow to God to liberate his land. The Latin *cruciata* is defined as "having been crucified."[4] Politics, business contracts among the Crusades' leaders, power struggles, and greed all factored into the bizarre attack of Catholic Christians from the West on transplanted Catholic Christians in Zara. Grace Young, writing for *Britannica*, comments, "It foreshadowed the same army's assault on Constantinople."[5]

Looking at firsthand sources gives us a glimpse of actions in the name of Christianity, directly and indirectly reflecting on Scripture. The following is from Choniates's eyewitness account:

Such then, to make a long story short, were the outrageous crimes committed by the Western armies against the inheritance of Christ. Without showing any feelings of humanity whatsoever, they exacted from all their money and chattel, dwellings and clothing, leaving to them nothing of all their goods. Thus behaved the brazen neck, the haughty spirit, the high brow, the ever-shaved and youthful cheek, the blood-thirsty right hand, the wrathful nostril, the disdainful eye, the insatiable jaw, the hateful heart, the piercing and running speech practically dancing over the lips.[6]

The massive force of European Christians reached Constantinople in 1202. By 1204, they did what the rest of the world's forces could not—conquered Constantinople, the seat of the Greek Orthodox Church and capital of Byzantium. At least an entire generation of Greek Christians lost their home, as the Greeks did not retake the city and restore Byzantium until 1261. The city defenses were so immense that the crusaders failed at first. After becoming distraught, they were ordered to listen to their bishops' sermons, which:

> Showed to the pilgrims that the war was a righteous one; for the Greeks were traitors and murderers, and also disloyal, since they had murdered their rightful lord, and were worse than Jews. Moreover, the bishops said that, by the authority of God and in the name of the pope, they would absolve all who attacked the Greeks. Then the bishops commanded the pilgrims to confess their sins and receive the communion devoutly; and said that they ought not to hesitate to attack the Greeks, for the latter were enemies of God. They also commanded that all the evil women should be sought out and sent away from the army to a distant place. This was done; the evil women were all put on a vessel and were sent very far away from the army.[7]

These sermons invoked biblical orders, as well as an expressly Catholic interpretation of Scriptures that endorsed indulgences. The use of "in the name of the pope" hints at Innocent III's earlier promise to absolve their sins.

Somehow, the invaders conquered the great city in spite of the mammoth obstacles. The three layers and levels of walls (plus a moat) were unparalleled at that time. The inner wall was an impressive twenty-feet thick and forty-feet tall. There were ninety-six towers, each one sixty-five-feet tall and forty-five-feet thick. Yet the structure could not withstand Constantinople's fellow Christians. Choniates summarizes its once-glorious streets after the sack:

> No one was without a share in the grief. In the alleys, in the streets, in the temples, complaints, weeping, lamentations, grief, the groaning of men, the shrieks of women, wounds, rape, captivity, the separation of those most closely united. Nobles wandered about ignominiously, those of venerable age in tears, the rich in poverty. Thus it was in the streets, on the corners, in the temple, in the dens, for no place remained unassailed or defended the suppliants. All places everywhere were filled full of all kinds of crime. Oh, immortal God, how great the afflictions of the men, how great the distress![8]

From Constantine's fourth-century legacy to the thirteenth century, the city had remained a stronghold. The city would last another two hundred years until finally succumbing to the Ottomans in 1453. Within this expansive defensive structure, and with a long heritage of being a Christian enclave in hostile lands, it would have appeared that the city would last until the end of time, being steeped in religious heritage with ties to Constantine who had called for the Council of Nicaea (AD 325) and Theodosius I, grandfather of the great wall builder, who made Christianity the empire's official religion.

Pope Innocent III himself later apologized for his ordered Crusade and excommunicated the combatants, despite later absolving them since their efforts enabled Rome to control both halves of Christendom. Centuries later, Pope John Paul II, perhaps the most popular pope of the post-Reformation era, apologized for this Crusade's massacre of Eastern Christians at Constantinople. On June 29, 2004, he stated to Bartholomew I, head of the three hundred million Greek Orthodox Christians: "In particular, we cannot forget what happened in the month of April 1204. . . . How can we not share, at a distance of eight centuries, the pain and disgust."[9]

It took three days for the Catholic crusaders to pillage Constantinople and permanently split Eastern and Western Christianity. Though Pope Innocent III eventually changed his mind, his harsh words and vivid descriptions are part of the permanent account of the evil carried out in his name and under the banner of Christianity. This is from his letter to his own legate:

> How, indeed, is the Greek church to be brought back into ecclesiastical union and to a devotion for the Apostolic See when she has been beset with so many afflictions and persecutions that she sees in the Latins only an example of perdition and the works of darkness, so that she now, and with reason, detests the Latins more than dogs? As for those who were supposed to be seeking the ends of Jesus Christ, not their own ends, whose swords, which they were supposed to use against the pagans, are now dripping with Christian blood they have spared neither age nor sex. They have committed incest, adultery, and fornication before the eyes of men. They have exposed both matrons and virgins, even those dedicated to God, to the sordid lusts of boys. Not satisfied with breaking open the imperial treasury and plundering the goods of princes and lesser men, they also laid their hands on the treasures of

the churches and, what is more serious, on their very possessions. They have even ripped silver plates from the altars and
have hacked them to pieces among themselves. They violated
the holy places and have carried off crosses and relics.[10]

Evil and suffering in the Fourth Crusade were the result of biblical
proof texting and, in this case, a militant use of the Catholic doctrine
of penance. Attached to it is the practice of indulgence. *Penance* (from
Latin *poenitentia,* akin to *paenitentia,* which means "regret") is generally defined as an action performed to show repentance or sorrow for
sin. When St. Jerome translated the Bible into Latin (the Vulgate), he
chose *penance* as a rendering of the New Testament words that actually denote *repentance.* Many non-Catholic scholars contend that this
was an error of monumental importance. Penance is an outward act,
whereas repentance is an inward act.

St. Jerome's translation of penance, according to most Protestant
scholars, radically altered the foundational doctrine of salvation. In
large part, it's also what prompted Martin Luther's challenge to some
fundraising practices among Catholics due to their creation of indulgences, which Protestants argue is a tenuous practice at best. In the
Roman Catholic Church and Eastern Orthodox (and some Anglican)
Church, a confessor (a local priest) listens to a sinner's confession,
administers absolution (the remission of the guilt or consequences
of the sin confessed), and then chooses and assigns the appropriate
penance.

An indulgence is a Roman Catholic practice of granting official
pardon (remission) of sins based on the belief that, after one sins
and the guilt has been forgiven, a debt is owed to God. The Roman
Catholic Church claims authority to grant such a remission because
of its apostolic succession, which it traces to St. Peter.[11] As George

Brantl and other Catholic scholars articulate, the Roman Catholic Church sees itself as being the Body of Christ on earth, and with this comes the power to grant indulgences.[12] This ties to a principle in Catholic teachings known as *vicarious satisfaction*, allegedly made possible through the spiritual treasury endowed by surplus merits of Christ, his mother Mary, and the saints. Other Catholic doctrines are related to this, such as *merits* (the reward for acts done in God's name and for God's glory) and papal decrees or bulls.[13]

All these doctrines are related to the unfolding of the Fourth Crusade debacle. Perhaps the following clarification helps with the repentance-penance differences:

> The true NT [New Testament] idea of repentance is very difficult to express in other languages. The Latin versions render *metanoeo* by *poenitentiam agere* ("exercise penitence"). But "penitence" etymologically signifies "pain, grief, distress," rather than a change of thought and purpose. Thus there developed in Latin Christianity a tendency to present grief over sin rather than abandonment of sin as the primary idea of NT repentance. . . . But the exhortations of the ancient prophets, of Jesus, and of the apostles show that the change of mind is the dominant idea of the words employed, while the accompanying grief and reform of life are necessary consequences.[14]

Perhaps the most articulate challenge or explanation of the Protestant response here is that of Martin Luther himself, a former Catholic priest, who says:

> No one can know whether the remission of sins is complete, because remission is granted only to those who exhibit worthy

contrition and confession, and no one can know whether contrition and confession are perfectly worthy. To assert that the pope can deliver souls from purgatory is audacious. If he can do so, then he is cruel not to release them all. But if he possesses this ability, he is in a position to do more for the dead than for the living. The purchasing of indulgences in any case is highly dangerous and likely to induce complacency. Indulgences can remit only those private satisfactions imposed by the Church, and may easily militate against interior penance, which consists in true contrition, true confession, and true satisfaction in spirit."[15]

The esteemed R. C. Sproul captures with enthusiasm the experience for Luther in his studies that underpins his above assessments and his approach to theology overall. Luther's conclusions are based on a reading of Romans 1:17, which is often credited with changing the course of history, or, at the least, launching the Protestant Reformation:

He says, "Here in *it*," in the gospel, "the righteousness of God is revealed from faith to faith, as it is written, 'the just shall live by faith.'" A verse taken from the book of Habakkuk in the Old Testament that is cited three times in the New Testament. As Luther would stop short and say, "What does this mean, that there's this righteousness that is by faith, and from faith to faith? What does it mean that the righteous shall live by faith?" Which again as I said was the thematic verse for the whole exposition of the gospel that Paul sets forth here in the book of Romans. And so, the lights came on for Luther. And he began to understand that what Paul was speaking of here was a righteousness that God in His grace was making available to those who would receive it passively, not those who would achieve it actively, but that would receive it by faith, and by which a person could be reconciled to a holy and righteous God.[16]

The success of the Crusades was inextricably linked to the pilgrims' belief in penance, papal decrees, indulgences, and various related doctrines. This was not merely an emotional campaign. People believed in spiritual blessings and in eternal rewards enough to risk their lives and resources and to sacrifice years of their time and energy.

Regardless of one's personal opinion regarding these Catholic doctrines, we must face the facts that they were grossly misused in the Fourth Crusade. The leaders withheld the papal order not to attack Christians. Instead, the crusaders were told to attack them with Pope Innocent III's blessings. The papal legate that Innocent III chastised, excerpted above, had taken it upon himself to offer absolution for the pilgrims' sins. In other words, the legate misrepresented the Pope's administrative, religious, and doctrinal authority. The crusaders' priests invoked divine orders to attack Christians inside the walls. The rationale is cloudy as it involves a faint spiritual connection to their political rejection of their Greek ruler. In the end, the irony is that biblical authority was used in Constantinople to depose a Catholic king and a papal vassal in an otherwise Greek Orthodox city.

The Fourth Crusade, along with other major and minor crusades, contained well-documented failures of Christian character. The rapacious acts, violence as mercenaries for others' political gains, looting, and a variety of mistakes have called the very use of the term *Crusades* into question in modern history. Many K–12 schools, often Christian, have changed their mascots from crusader imagery to tamer and less controversial subjects—often animals. The same has happened at the college level. In fact, one of my alma maters, Wheaton College (Illinois), changed its nickname from the Wheaton "Crusaders" to the Wheaton "Thunder" in 2000. Perhaps the most noticeable forfeiture of the name was by Campus Crusade for Christ, which changed its name to Cru in 2011. Though its original name reflected the large "crusade" revivals of the past, such as those Billy Graham presented across the country, many believed it carried "too many negative associations."[17]

IS THE BIBLE AT FAULT?

The Biblical Outcome

The misuse of the Bible in the Crusades is a bit more muted than it is in some of our other topics, but it's still there if we know where to look for it. When certain popes called for Crusades, they did so with the express intent to free Jerusalem and the holy land from the control of non-Christian rulers. Psalm 122:6 is a key verse in this regard, as it urges prayer for the peace of Jerusalem and promises security to those who love Jerusalem. In some respects, the crusaders saw themselves as fulfilling the descriptions in Zechariah 14, in which the Lord would oppose the nations who had gathered in Jerusalem to pillage it. The crusaders believed themselves to be God's army sent to fight at Jerusalem, and, because of this, many thought they were entitled to "the wealth of all the surrounding nations" mentioned in Zechariah 14:14.

As a symbol, the cross was front and center throughout the Crusades. It was worn on shields and armor and featured on flags and processional objects as a kind of unofficial logo for all crusading exploits. It was presented as a declaration of divine authority and worn as a sign of protection. Many crusaders swore allegiance to the cross of Christ and to ensuring that Christ was proclaimed to the nations. Any who didn't accept this proclamation were at risk of being attacked and treated as enemies of God, just like those enemies we see in books like Joshua or Revelation.

Point of Departure from Biblical Orthodoxy

Biblical orthodoxy offers zero justification for the senseless killing of innocent noncombatants. The murder of fellow Christians adds another layer to this abuse. We shouldn't overlook Paul's call in Romans

12:10, to "Love one another with brotherly affection. Outdo one another in showing honor." In 1 Corinthians 6:1–8, the apostle further argues that Christians shouldn't even harm each other by issuing lawsuits against a brother in Christ. These acts of violence against God's family would be grounds for divine reproach, such as what God offered through the prophets to the leaders over Israel who had harmed their own people.

Furthermore, the issue of greed was one of the key motivations behind the attack at Zara, mentioned early in this chapter. The Bible condemns greed in all its many forms. Christians are to be on guard against all forms of greed (Luke 12:15) and cannot serve both God and money (Matthew 6:24). The crusaders' refusal to accept the surrender of the people at Zara is also at odds with Scripture, as Deuteronomy 20:10–11 explicitly instructs invading armies to offer terms of peace before they attack, and then to accept the peace if the doors are opened. Attacking a city that has already surrendered simply to obtain its goods is an outright rejection of these clear biblical commands.

Problem Type

One of the crusaders' biggest problems was their blind allegiance to governing authorities and supposed divine mandates. They accepted these "facts" without examining the consequences. Submission to leaders is important in the Bible—except when those leaders are violating the instructions God has given. Paul urges us to "be subject to the governing authorities" in Romans 13:1. However, using biblical texts to endorse seizing lands and goods is also a clear misuse of biblical texts. As we've seen before, some of the most dangerous rhetoric is cloaked in religious language about the will of God. Identifying any distorted cause with the will of God lends it a level of authority that has the potential to result in wide-ranging and horrific consequences.

In this regard, we would do well to remember that it is God's will that none perish but all receive eternal life (2 Peter 3:9). Any leader who espouses ideas to the contrary is actually opposing the character of God, who is "merciful and gracious, slow to anger, and abounding in steadfast love and faithfulness" (Exodus 34:6). Using violence for personal gain or to try to force conversion is indefensible from a biblical perspective.

ANTIDOTE

One antidote to the crusaders' violent abuses would be the instructions in 1 John 4:1–6 to "test the spirits to see whether they are from God, for many false prophets have gone out into the world." Rather than accept a leader's instructions to attack Christian cities or slaughter Muslim inhabitants, those receiving such instructions could have "tested the spirits" to see if the orders were from God. Would the actions further God's kingdom by offering the gospel to all without force?

In many regards, the act of wearing the cross into battle was not unlike the acts of Hophni and Phineas to take the Ark of the Covenant into battle as a talisman that would ensure their protection (1 Samuel 4:1–11). The Ark, in fact, did not signify God was fighting for the Israelites that day; neither did the image of the cross mean that God was fighting for the crusaders. They would have done well to learn from the story in 1 Samuel 4–6 that God does not like being treated as an object of protection and does not depend on a human army to display his dominance over all other deities. This is clear in that same biblical account, as God broke the Philistine god Dagon and sent plagues among the Philistines themselves for defiling the Ark of the

Covenant (1 Samuel 6). God also does not need an army to liberate his people, as we see perfectly demonstrated in the Israelites' exodus from Egypt (Exodus 7–14).

Another antidote to exerting force like the crusaders is to pray and allow God to work. The Psalms provide a good illustration of what this entails. In Psalm 54, the psalmist describes how strangers have been ruthless in seeking to end the psalmist's life. Rather than acting in violence and amassing an army to liberate others, the psalmist puts hope in God and petitions God to repay the evil and deliver him from trouble. The superscription offers a context for the psalm as being during the time when an entire city of Ziphites betrayed David and wanted to hand him over to Saul, despite how Saul was hunting his own son-in-law without cause. Rather than repaying violence with violence, the antidote involves praying to God and extending love even to one's enemies.

Whenever Christians are attacking Christians, something is amiss. The story of the Fourth Crusade is difficult on so many levels. The reality that a military force willingly attacked its allies is mindboggling. The reality that soldiers and victims both held on to the message of the cross is tragic—not that they held it, but that the assailants recognized its form but not its function. They recognized its shape but not its spiritual purpose, which led to victims on all sides. We see in the papal apologies for this Crusade that time helps to heal, and throughout the journey of civilizations the Bible's message doesn't change, only our perspective.

For in it the righteousness of God is revealed from faith
for faith, as it is written, "The righteous shall live by faith."
ROMANS 1:17

Therefore, since we have been justified by faith, we have peace
with God through our Lord Jesus Christ. Through him
we have also obtained access by faith into this grace in which
we stand, and we rejoice in hope of the glory of God.
ROMANS 5:1–2

But God, being rich in mercy, because of the great love
with which he loved us, even when we were dead
in our trespasses, made us alive together with Christ. . . .
For by grace you have been saved through faith.
And this is not your own doing; it is the gift of God,
not a result of works, so that no one may boast.
EPHESIANS 2:4–5, 8–9

CHAPTER 12

The Degradation of Australia's Aborigines:

Why Misreading a Passage
Might Displace a People

Then you shall drive out all the inhabitants of the land
from before you and destroy all their figured stones and destroy
all their metal images and demolish all their high places.
And you shall take possession of the land and settle in it,
for I have given the land to you to possess it.

NUMBERS 33:52–53

He said, "Cursed be Canaan; a servant of servants
shall he be to his brothers."

GENESIS 9:25

The story of Britain transporting criminals to the land down under in 1788 is often told as Australia's founding. Tell that to the Aborigines, whose long, proud history predates Britain's arrival by at least fifty thousand years.[1] Since many Europeans didn't consider these "blacks" to be human beings, their ostensible Christianization of the outback was deemed permissible either by design or default. As the common colonialization argument went, taking advantage of the wonderful resources of Australia was part of a divine mandate; providence willed it. Though Australians later labeled their settlers' actions as inhumane, the pogroms decimated the indigenous people of Australia, especially the full-blooded Tasmanian Aborigines who became extinct by the end of the so-called "great" missionary century.

Writing with a close-up view in 1870, Christian historian James Bonwick's words penetrate even a century later: "We cover our faces while the deep and solemn voice of our common Father echoes through the soul, 'where is thy brother?'"[2] Few white settlers, let alone missionaries, saw what missionary William Ridley did in the mid-nineteenth century. The Aborigines' spirituality led them to believe that they were God-seeking people with "a thirst for religious mystery."[3]

By the middle of the nineteenth century, all mission efforts from all denominations had given up on the Aborigines. It is of little surprise since many religious leaders saw them as irredeemable savages. Consider the following words from Presbyterian missionary Thomas Dove and legendary (and controversial) Anglican minister, Samuel Marsden. Dove concludes that the Aborigines lacked all moral values, and "such is their depth of degradation that they have reached the level of the beasts."[4] In a letter to another minister in 1819, Marsden, the senior cleric of New South Wales, surmises that Aborigines were the "most degraded of the human race" and not capable of being civilized. Perhaps as troubling is his notion that they were not ready "to receive the knowledge of Christianity."[5] Most of the missionaries tolerated a warped ethnocentrism that prompted educated people to believe that *superior* races were the design of Providence, and so was the justification for the removal or passing of *inferior* races. William Hull, in an official hearing before the Select Committee of Victoria, and in response to a question about the lone survivor of Tasmanian Aborigines (a widow), gave this callous response: "We must come to the conclusion that the beneficent Creator never intended Tasmania to be a permanent home of the savage, but to be filled with a free, an honest, a peaceful people."[6] How peaceful, though, is a people that roasts children and their families alive, tortures and slaughters them in sport, and steals all of their possessions? That was the example set by the British.

In 1804, just one year after Australia's second penal settlement began at Hobart Town, Aborigine families were massacred while traveling together for their annual hunting expeditions. At least fifty were slaughtered at the mouth of the Derwent River near Risdon Cove, and the "Risdon Massacre" became a stain on British expansionism— not to mention a testament to Christian apathy. In the years ahead, the Aborigines who were:

> Simply shot were fortunate. Many were cruelly tortured, maimed, blinded, burnt, and castrated. The evidence in official documents is horrifying enough without guessing at that which was never divulged. They were shot for dogs' meat. Women were chained to the huts of white settlers, used by the men, then tortured to death, with some being forced to wear the heads of their murdered husbands.[7]

In less than thirty years, the white Europeans killed 90 percent of the four thousand Aborigines around Hobart Town.[8]

There is resurgent interest today among many Australians in honoring the Aborigines and recognizing their unjust plight. Some token expressions include the two optional celebrations offered to off-set the anniversary of 1788, or Australia Day. Television station NITV established the first option, Invasion Day, to commemorate "a time of mourning by Aboriginal peoples for all that was lost subsequent to that event." A second option is Survival Day, which "recognizes the vitality of Australia's diverse Indigenous cultures *despite* coloniza-tion"—popularized by Sydney's Yabun Festival.[9]

With this resurgence of support for the nearly decimated indig-enous peoples, it's a good time to explore questions about the use and misuse of the Bible in their journeys. The early British settlers claimed Numbers 33:52–53, seeing themselves as the Israelites and the Aborigines as the Canaanites:

Then you shall drive out all the inhabitants of the land from before you and destroy all their figured stones and destroy all their metal images and demolish all their high places. And you shall take possession of the land and settle in it, for I have given the land to you to possess it.

John Harris, the main source for our study, was a lifelong mission-ary and friend of the Aborigines. While he was president of the Zadok Institute for Christianity and Society, he addressed the Europeans' ra-pacious actions head-on in *Zadok Perspectives*. Against the backdrop of the errant theology of the Hamite curse on the African (black) peoples—based on the curse on Noah's son, Ham (Genesis 9:25 and 10:6)—he states:

I am not saying that the Christian church ever sanctioned the murder of Aboriginal people, but the church failed miserably for a century or more to stand publicly against the oppression of the original inhabitants of the land. Nineteenth century Christians have generally convinced themselves that in the eternal scheme of things, the Aborigines were the Canaanites in the day, the Europeans, the Israelites. William Hull wrote a whole book in 1846 demonstrating that Aborigines were the "degraded descendants of the nations driven out by the divine command to the uttermost parts of the earth, and to the islands beyond the seas."[10]

As we look closer at the early nineteenth century, we will find it even more amazing that many Aborigines are leaders in today's churches. In fact, 73 percent of Aborigines (and Torres Strait Islander peoples) self-report as Christians—more than the rest of Australians, who self-report at 61 percent.[11] However, questions remain. "Aboriginal and Torres Strait Islanders have a bittersweet relationship with the church, and for good reason. Their living memories include loss of language and culture, and even direct experience as the Stolen Generation—as well as, often, a sacred space of refuge and connection with God."[12]

In 1853, Lancelot Threlkeld, a Congregational missionary who gave much of his life to translating the Bible for the Aborigines, reflected on the European Christians' mistreatment of the Aborigines. He had previously delved into language translation and, in 1830, produced the first translation of the Bible in an Aboriginal language (the Gospel of Luke in Awabakal). Twenty-two years after this translation (and much disillusioned with the London Missionary Society for what he perceived was ignoring acute needs of a disenfranchised and abused people), he writes:

It was maintained by many of the colony that the blacks had no language at all but were only a race of the monkey tribe. This was a convenient assumption, for if it could be proved that the Aborigines . . . were only a species of wild beasts, there could be no guilt attributed to those who shot them off or poisoned them.[13]

During the same decade of his translation, the *Sydney Herald* (and other Australian papers) regularly published comments that corroborate Threlkeld's assessment, totally dehumanizing the Aborigines, such as one calling them:

. . . the most degenerate, despicable and brutal race of beings in existence, and stand as it were in scorn to "shame creation"— a scoff and a jest upon humanity, they are insensible to every bond which binds man to his friend: husband to wife, parent to its child or creature to its God.[14]

Many of the published comments are reminiscent of the racism before, during, and after American slavery. A juror in an 1838 trial of seven white men who massacred twenty-eight blacks, including whole families, commented afterward in the *Australian*: "I look on the blacks as a set of monkeys, and the earlier they are exterminated from the face of the earth the better."[15] He also noted he knew the whites were guilty but would never convict them for killing blacks.

Contradictions abound here in the white Australians' logic to suppress the Aborigines. During the same year that Threlkeld finished his gospel translation, the *Sydney Gazette* published the obituary of perhaps the most famous Aborignal, "Majesty King BOONGARIE, Supreme

Chief of the Sydney tribe,"[16] today often referred to as Bungaree. A decade before his death, the governor named Boongaree Island in his honor, and today the suburb of Bongaree, Queensland attests to his legacy. But the obituary has the veneer of praise for him, "the most renowned of his tribe":

> The facetiousness of the sable chief, and the superiority of his mental endowments, over those of the generality of his race, obtained for him a more than ordinary share of regard from the white inhabitants of the colony. . . . Boongarie was remarkable for his partiality for the English costume; and it must be confessed that his appearance was sometimes grotesque enough, when he had arrayed his person in such "shreds and patches" of coats and nether garments as he could by any means obtain; the whole surmounted by an old cocked hat, with "the humour of forty fancies pricked in't for a feather."[17]

Keep this obituary in mind as you read below about the inhumane treatment of Bungaree's people during the very time the newspaper gave this hint of applause. Some are clapping for his theatrical acts while others were killing his extended family in the grossest of manners.

The atrocities the Aborigines faced across Australia have brought tears to my eyes on more than one occasion. I have visited their country several times and was once even given a private tour of the country's oldest church, which included priceless Bibles and photographs—considered by some to be national treasures. However, it was my research for this book that brought the harsh realities of the nineteenth-century slaughter before me in vivid detail. The settlers' unjust actions—including some missionaries' active participation and the passive silence of others—are among the worst actions by Christian groups in recorded history.

John Harris's 956-page tome, *One Blood: 200 Years of Aboriginal Encounter with Christianity—A Story of Hope,* provides enough primary documents to validate what is told in passing elsewhere. One particularly tough section of this book refers to Threlkeld's 1837 annual report. It captures the essence of this pogrom, but the following is not for the faint of heart:

> A war of extirpation [had] long existed, in which the ripping open of the bellies of the blacks alive; the roasting of them in that state in triangularly made log fires, made for the very purpose; the dashing of infants upon the stones; the confining of a party in a hut and letting them out singly through the doorway, to be butchered as they endeavoured to escape, together with many other atrocious acts of cruelty, which are but the sports of monsters boasting of superior intellect to that possessed by the wretched blacks![18]

Threlkeld's personal journey is heroic, befitting his first name—Lancelot. His was a missionary life dogged by the inhumane actions of other missionaries against the very natives he was helping. It appears that his strong presence and personality may have put him at odds with many, and he shifted from the London Missionary Society to private funders. Contemporary accounts note that the hard life had taken its toll on his formerly strong physique, which is noticeable in pictures throughout his career. His sense of disillusionment with institutionalized Christianity amidst the horrific treatment of the Aborigines also had a negative impact on his Bible translation and led to the closing of his ten-thousand-acre mission in Ebenezer.

Both casualties were tied to the stark reality that only a few Awabakal speakers were left—the foreigners had killed most of them and introduced alcohol to the few who remained. Threlkeld's translation wasn't published until 1892, but more out of curiosity than for actual use. In 1941, the local governor finally closed his mission.

A deep sense of frustration is evident in Threlkeld's 1837 report, which was meant "to express concern that so many years of constant attention appear to have been fruitlessly expended." He directly comments on the foreigners' systematic and guiltless pogrom:

> It is, however, perfectly apparent that the termination of the Mission has arisen solely from the Aborigines becoming extinct in these districts and the very few that remain elsewhere are so scattered. . . . The thousands of Aborigines . . . decreased to hundreds, the hundreds have lessened to tens, and the tens will dwindle into units, before a very few years shall have passed away.[19]

Through the decades since the exemplary missionary zeal of Threlkeld, many gracious, selfless, Bible-centered missionary efforts have spread throughout the region. Many of the Aborigines have accepted apologies for the past sins of early settlers. Perhaps chief among these is Archbishop Grindrod on behalf of the Anglican Church to Aboriginal Bishop Arthur Malcolm. Missions and Christian efforts have returned in recent decades with a revitalized partnership and mutual respect between the Aborigines and Christian missionaries. Revivals have occurred, infused by the "Black Crusade" of Echo Island in 1979 and the "Miracle Days at Mt. Margaret" in 1982.[20]

The theme throughout these revivals and up to present day is the leadership of indigenous Christians. The transition "from mission to church" may sound trite, but it sums up this delayed acceptance of the gospel. Harris concludes, "It is hard to find a better phrase to describe that transition which marks the end of subordination and the beginning of autonomy."[21]

Near the end of his invaluable tome on the plight of the Aborigines, *One Blood,* which has been consulted heavily for this discussion, John Harris offers the wonderful reminders of both the human dynamic of their story and the standalone nature of the Bible itself. The revivals and real commitment came to the Aborigines as they began to see themselves as partners with—rather than clients of—the white Europeans. And curiously, though not surprisingly, the hero of the Aborigines at Roper River became James Noble. He was the first ordained Aboriginal person, despite never being allowed to become a priest. He is credited with introducing Roper River to the gospel. And, on biblical authority, Harris closes his discussion with John 4:14, "But whoever drinks of the water that I will give him will never be thirsty again. The water that I will give him will become in him a spring of water welling up to eternal life."[22]

IS THE BIBLE AT FAULT?

The Biblical Outcome

More than its reading of a given text, the Australian abuse of Aboriginal peoples was motivated by an interest in taking land that didn't belong to them. In an age of colonization and imperialist expansion, Australia's Aborigines weren't looking to expand but to continue to stay in the same territory—longer than any other people had done. They could boast of one of the world's longest continuous cultures. But these distinctions didn't negate the harsh reality of European expansion, and that this indigenous people was standing in the way of *progress* and *expansion*. The most useful Bible texts for many colonizers were passages like Numbers 33:53. This verse was spoken to the Israelites as they were about to enter Canaan; it doesn't have anything to do with the expansion of the British Empire or its colonies. But the tendency throughout history for white Europeans to identify themselves with the biblical Israelites allows for passages like this to be co-opted and abused. By identifying themselves with the Israelites, the colonists identified the Aborigines with the Canaanites and thereby misused other Old Testament passages regarding that people. So, when they were accused of barbarism, the colonists labeled their atrocities as *divine judgment*. Their horrific penchant for bashing babies against rocks could be wrongly justified by relating it to Psalm 137:7–9, in which David mentions this slaughter as retribution for the Edomites doing the same to Israelite babies.

The curse of Ham, which we noted in the previous chapter, was also connected with the seizure of the homes of Aborigines. The reasoning went that, if these "black" Aborigines were descended from Ham, they were meant to be slaves; they were meant to be *owned as property*, rather than being *owners of property*. And, as we noted, the idea was that Ham and his descendants were cursed by Noah to be the slaves of Shem, Japheth, and their descendants. Naturally, Shem and Japheth were claimed as ancestors by many white European missionaries; this gave them the right to subjugate and abuse the sons of Ham, or Hamites, they encountered.

Colonists also used verses like John 4:14, in which Jesus refers to himself as *living water*, to justify their crimes. If the Aborigines rejected the living water Jesus offered, they reasoned, then death was what awaited them.

Point of Departure from Biblical Orthodoxy

Edward Parker, ex-protector and member of the Victorian Legislative Council, reminds young Christians of the evil consequences of using flawed logic and a misuse of Scripture. The "common notion" that the Aborigines are "a doomed race" and that "they must pass" runs counter to biblical precepts:

> Nay, the opinion assumes a more daring form in the asser-
> tion that it is an appointment—the inscrutable decree—of
> Divine Providence that uncivilized races should perish before
> the march of civilization. . . . I want to know where the decree
> is written. . . . Do you not see that if the argument be worth
> anything that, if followed out to its ultimate consequences,
> it can be made to justify every outrage, and to palliate every
> crime?—God has suffered it, and therefor he wills it![23]

We find in Parker a passionate advocate for the Aborigines, calling "every Christian man rise and say with one voice" to all the authorities, "occupy the land, till its broad wastes; extract its riches, develop its re-sources, if you will; but, in the name of God and humanity, *Save the people.*"[24] Fortunately, some listened.

The incredible volume, *Our Mob, God's Story: Aboriginal and Torres Strait Islander Artists Share Their Faith,* highlights the cause's new champions. The editors of this work, a finalist for the 2017 Christian Book Award (ECPA), intend this project "to aid the process of recon-ciliation between Aboriginal and non-Aboriginal Australians."[25] This volume, representing the Bible Society Australia, honors the words of the apostle Paul in 2 Corinthians 5:18, "All this is from God, who through Christ reconciled us to himself and gave us the ministry of reconciliation."[26]

The idea that the Aborigines were beyond saving flies in the face of the biblical idea that all can repent and embrace God's offer of salvation. Consider the conversion of Romans who had fed Christians to wild beasts and slaughtered people in masses; how could people like that be converted while one of the longest-settled and most peaceful people groups in the world be beyond help? Even the apostle Paul committed numerous "barbaric" crimes against Christians before his encounter with Christ on the road to Damascus. Jesus softened Paul's heart and commissioned him as a missionary whose example and selfless sharing of the gospel may represent Christianity's most famous conversion. In his letter to the Colossians, Paul declares that in Christ "there is not Greek and Jew, circumcised and uncircumcised, barbarian, Scythian, slave, [or] free" (Colossians 3:11). So, this idea that Aborigines were too barbaric to receive the gospel loses all biblical footing.

Problem Type

As we diagnose this abuse of the Bible as a type we might quote John Harris from his paper on Aboriginal land rights:

I have emphasized this false reconstruction of reality at some length because it is a stern warning to us all. It is far too easy to read into scripture that which we want to see, to use scripture selectively to sanctify our own ambitions, or those of our own social class, or nation. This is a clear case of such an abuse of scripture here in Australia, and further more, in connection with the very matter we are discussing—the rights of the Aboriginal people.[27]

The abuses that were committed by Australian colonists against native peoples are, hopefully, largely irrelevant to our own relationship to the Bible. Few of us are inclined to use other humans for target practice or engage in wars of extermination. The underlying problem, though, is one we're all faced with: embracing and following ethical and moral standards. While the atrocities of the Aboriginal genocide seem distant from the choices we make today, throughout our lives we're challenged with our reaction to and support of things that either lead to good or to harmful or destructive ends. Ultimately, the allegiance of our hearts belongs to God

Any quote or literature can be used to justify violence, and the stakes are raised when the Bible is involved. Not only does the Bible contain violent passages that can be misused and taken out of context, its claims of divine authority can be exploited to magnify anything that goes wrong.

Even some well-meaning missionaries gave up on the Aborigines when they didn't convert. They accepted the idea that it was impossible for God to change the hearts of certain people. In doing so, they ignored the hope intrinsic in Christianity that "with God all things are possible" (Matthew 19:26). When the missionaries stepped away from their mission field, the Aborigines were more vulnerable than ever and found themselves, in many cases, without protection from the other foreigners.

ANTIDOTE

In many ways, the conclusions of Bartolomé de Las Casas offer an important corrective to acts of conquest by Christians. Las Casas was a Spanish Dominican priest sent as a missionary to the Americas in the mid-sixteenth century. Upon his arrival, he witnessed the abuses of the colonizing conquistadors against the native inhabitants and wrote letters to the king of Spain requesting that these abuses be stopped. Sound familiar? Same ethical issues that were mishandled in Australia. Same Bible averted. Once again, forceful oppressors claiming some warped sense of divine favor. His work, *In Defense of the Indians*, asserts that one "cannot be forced to a religion neither can one be forced to hear the dogmas and traditions of a religion."[28] Force is antithetical to the gospel. Responsible Bible reading cannot justify oppression, greed, or self-elevation.

When misused and abused in these ways, the Bible is not at fault. It's instead the abusers who are to blame for joining those indicted by Peter for being "the ignorant and unstable [who] twist [the words] to their own destruction, as they do to the other Scriptures" (2 Peter 3:16).

Whoever oppresses a poor man insults his Maker,
but he who is generous to the needy honors him.
PROVERBS 14:31

Show yourself in all respects to be a model of good works,
and in your teaching show integrity, dignity, and sound speech
that cannot be condemned, so that an opponent may be
put to shame, having nothing evil to say about us.
TITUS 2:7–8

CONCLUSION
Biblical Standards
Identify Errant Scenarios

To the pure, all things are pure, but to the defiled
and unbelieving, nothing is pure;
but both their minds and their consciences are defiled.
They profess to know God, but they deny him by their works.
They are detestable, disobedient, unfit for any good work.

TITUS 1:15-16

Either by design or default, people have misused biblical teachings from the time they were first shared and then recorded. Many of the leaders of Israel were classified in the Bible itself as evil—and their very people and heritage inextricably tied to the story of God's favor. And sadly, masses have followed heresies and schemes. Besides the spiritual implications, these wayward efforts have often led to rather bizarre behavior and, even worse, evil and suffering.

While this phenomenon of co-opted religious texts isn't unique to Christianity, it is especially disconcerting because the theological stakes are so high. Either the Son of God became incarnate and walked this earth in the first century, or he didn't. Either Jesus was and is part of the divine Trinity, or he isn't. Either our eternal destiny rests on his actual life, death, and resurrection, or the whole shebang is an unfortunate ruse. There are no legitimate disclaimers of his historic presence, but many challenges to his *real* message.

If Jesus is not the Christ, Christianity's core is hollow. Given this maxim, countless heretics have presented vacuous versions of *veritas* (truth). We have creeds for a reason, in large part to affirm our core doctrines while exposing pretenders. If people tried to earn money or offer false teachings during earthly ministries of Christ and his apostles (Acts 8:14–24), then we should be little surprised that history has a steady stream of the same. Some people watched Jesus raise Lazarus from the dead and then still chose to conspire against him (John 11:45–53). We might conclude they saw the truth firsthand but rejected it, and some even chose to try to destroy it. In this light, the taxonomy of leaders offering corrupted doctrine isn't all that perplexing. They only know of Christ's message through his revealed word in the Bible, and in direct violation of it clear message, choose personal gain over its intended ends.

Biblical standards abound for both behavior and sound teaching, and each of our case studies reveals violations of one or both aspects. The apostle Paul gives clear advice about these matters to Titus for his work among the Cretans. He warns him about "debauchery" and "insubordination." For the selection of church leaders or "overseer," they "must be above reproach" and "not be arrogant or quick-tempered or a drunkard or violent or greedy for gain" (Titus 1:5–7). Paul isn't simply concerned about a leader failing in *all* of these areas; he teaches that failure in any *one* would disqualify someone for Christian leadership. And yet, some of the leaders of bizarre and often destructive teachings we discussed seem to fill the entire checklist of Paul's disqualifiers.

Arrogance and greed, just two of a longer list, should have knocked a few of our wayward leaders out of the running. The string of Cadillacs, opulent lifestyle, and shakedown offerings at Oriole Theater did not bode well for Prophet Jones, the Messiah in Mink. The fancy robes and gold hair weaves alone may have disqualified Tanchelm—and that's not even counting his ploy to increase offerings by marrying a statue of the Virgin Mary! Jan of Leiden certainly couldn't be considered "above reproach"; his actions put him well below it. The preoccupation with money and power also disqualified the leaders of the Fourth Crusade.

The other aspect of Paul's charge to Titus is sound or orthodox teaching. Even had the leaders above had solid character, their unsound teaching should have been challenged extensively. Paul continues with his advice to Titus:

> For there are many who are insubordinate, empty talkers and deceivers, especially those of the circumcision party. They must be silenced, since they are upsetting whole families by teaching for shameful gain what they ought not to teach. One of the Cretans, a prophet of their own, said, "Cretans are always liars, evil beasts, lazy gluttons." This testimony is true. Therefore rebuke them sharply, that they may be sound in the faith, not devoting themselves to Jewish myths and the commands of people who turn away from the truth. To the pure, all things are pure, but to the defiled and unbelieving, nothing is pure; but both their minds and their consciences are defiled. They profess to know God, but they deny him by their works. They are detestable, disobedient, unfit for any good work. (Titus 1:10-16)

We have painted against this backdrop of orthodoxy a few sketches of the Bible's misuses. Some of these misuses are more colorful than others, but all are tragic. Every misuse represented in these pages involved groups of people exerting considerable energies for heresies, scams, or both. We could have written volumes on these and similar cases. In each case we asked, *Is the Bible at fault?* And, in each case, the answer is No. People either slightly distorted Christ's messages or they completely corrupted them. They either practiced irresponsible hermeneutics with the Old Testament or refashioned New Testament passages to dress their own agendas.

Nearly a thousand mesmerized people gave their entire possessions to a messianic figure and joined him in Benton Harbor, Michigan. They believed his calculated message that the truly righteous would never experience physical death. Evidently, all but two have already failed the test, as two elderly members still hold out hope—allegedly, while their messianic founder lays embalmed in a nearby room.

The Phibionites were of "reprobate mind" (Romans 1:28 KJV) and grossly violated numerous biblical tenets. Self-mutilation and self-inflicted pain, including crucifixion reenactments, operated under a hyper-literalism. Handling snakes on the stage placed a tangential and problematic biblical text—not to mention the proven health risks—at the fulcrum of worship and membership. Several gifted preachers predicted Christ's return, even though the Bible warns against such actions. Some organizations like the Ku Klux Klan gave such radical, errant interpretations of biblical passages that even calling them biblical or Christian in any sense isn't warranted at all. And, in Australia, like in many other regions at different times, one race errantly claimed God's favor over another—with dire consequences.

The church could never have been built if we focused only on what was done in error. Instead, we depend on guidance from orthodox teaching and celebration for honorable actions. Paul reminds Titus, and all of us, that a leader should be "hospitable, a lover of good, self-controlled, upright, holy, and disciplined. He must hold firm to the trustworthy word as taught, so that he may be able to give instruction in sound doctrine and also to rebuke those who contradict it" (Titus 1:8–9).

Perhaps on occasion you will hear Jonah's story and think of the Klan's corrupted use for its own ends. Or, you'll pass a statue in a cathedral and wonder if it ever married a priest. When you hear a baby's rattle in the pew behind you, you'll think of the ending of Mark and how different your service is than 125 churches in Appalachia. Maybe, like me, you'll be driving past Benton Harbor, Michigan and take a detour to see the remains of a cult that left palatial buildings that arrest your attention. And that's the kicker: too often people confuse palaces here for ones eternal. And the next time you see an Aborigine's face, in person or portrait, you'll pause in awe of God's magnificent design of those in his image. In the recesses of your mind, you'll recall some of the horrific challenges to their very survival. But in the front of your mind you'll know we are all fearfully and wonderfully made.

ACKNOWLEDGEMENTS

I wish every author had the benefit of at least one project with a publishing house of Worthy's ilk. This is my third Worthy Publishing book in as many years, in large part because I thoroughly enjoy the team—and they aren't just that. They are gifted editors, friends, realists, and fans. They know that creativity is a job half done; helping writers like me to categorize and package ideas is a valued process. The visceral dynamic from the conception of an idea to commitment to a book is invaluable, and who better to have at the helm than Byron Williamson and Jeana Ledbetter? They have published thousands of books between them. Byron is also chair of the Evangelical Christian Publishing Association board, so he's the fulcrum of some rather wonderful projects. And Jeana was with Yates and Yates literary agency before joining Worthy, and it seems like everyone knows her.

These colleagues in the publishing journey have brought a special joy to the journey. Their associates, like Leeanna Nelson and Nicole Pavlas, complement the process with their professionalism and personalities. It's also in order to thank the coauthors of this book, Nicholas De Neff and Daniel Freemyer. Though I served as the text's main writer, these coauthors assisted with research, reviews, and edits. From trips to Benton Harbor, Michigan and logging library time, to interviews with key source persons like the indefatigable John Harris (Australia), they have certainly strengthened this book. Their recent seminary degrees were invaluable in framing the biblical interaction with errant practices.

Nearly all of my projects, including this one, benefit from my core writing team. These colleagues are Todd Ream (Taylor University) and Chris Devers (Johns Hopkins University). Their candid feedback and constant inspiration are part of a cherished routine—usually at Jax Café or Abbey Coffee in Marion, Indiana. A shout out to these shop owners—Jack Gardner and Darren Campbell. They welcome (and sometimes tolerate) us as we occupy their tables for hours with minimal purchases.

A special thanks to President David Wright and Provost Stacy Hammons at Indiana Wesleyan University. They lead an entrepreneurial educational home that has always supported my research and writing efforts. They also support intermittent hibernation with my books.

It is appropriate to end these acknowledgements while nodding to my family. During this book's journey, I appreciated the patience of Cindy and our four boys, Jason, Joshua, Nick, and Michael. They have often joked that they thought my laptop was an appendage.

NOTES

INTRODUCTION

1 Jerry Pattengale, "Kissing the Pavement in Vatican City," *Chronicle Tribune,* June 29, 2018.

2 See J. R. W. Stott, *Basic Christianity,* rev. ed. (Grand Rapids, MI: Wm. B. Eerdmans Publisher, 1971). One of the most robust efforts in recent history to help a large group of Christians understand the Bible is *The Africa Study Bible* (Tyndale House).

3 See Ben Witherington, III, *Reading and Understanding the Bible* (Oxford: Oxford University Press, 2014); Kenneth Schenck, *Making Sense of God's Word* (Indianapolis: Wesleyan Publishing House, 2009); and Richard B. Hays and Ellen F. Davis, eds., *The Art of Reading Scripture* (Grand Rapids, MI: Wm. B. Eerdmans, 2003).

4 One of the most respected sources for religious news in the secular space is the Religion News Service. *First Things,* founded in 1990 by Lutheran religious scholar, Richard John Neuhaus, is a leading conservative ecumenical journal. *Christianity Today,* founded in 1956 by religious leader Billy Graham, remains the respected source for features from a Christian evangelical perspective, with a growing digital presence. A more recent publication, *WORLD Magazine,* offers helpful pieces on a mélange of topics, also from a conservative perspective and with a breadth of delivery platforms. The Evangelical Christian Publishers Association is an active network collaborating for publishing and educational resources, and it monitors the annual Christian Book Awards, founded in 1978. The Society of Biblical Literature has over eight thousand members and claims it is "the largest international association of scholars who teach and research the variety of fields that make up biblical studies. SBL is an interdisciplinary, humanistic, academic society that includes scholars of history, literature, archaeology, anthropology, theology, and more" (https://www.sbl-site.org /aboutus/default.aspx). Numerous other organizations exist for similar purposes, all with their particular missions, e.g., Conference on Faith & History ("exploring the relationship between Christian faith and history"), European Leadership Forum, Evangelical Theological Society, Biblical Research Institute, Institute for Biblical Research, Baylor University's Institute for Studies of Religion, and higher education networks like Council for Christian Colleges and Universities (conservative Protestants) and Association of Catholic Colleges & Universities, both based in Washington, DC. Among the leading biblical textual study centers are Tyndale House (Cambridge), the Center for the Study of New Testament Manuscripts at Dallas Theological Seminary, and The Institute for New Testament Textual Research in Münster, Germany.

CHAPTER 1

1 John Carlisle, "Benton Harbor Remembers Cult Destroyed by Sex Scandal," *Detroit Free Press,* November 13, 2016, https://www.freep.com/story/news/columnists/john–carlisle/2016/11/13 /house–of–david–benton–harbor/93069448/.

2 Clare E. Adkin, *Brother Benjamin: A History of the Israelite House of David* (Berrien Springs, MI: Andrews University Press, 1990) 2.

3 The historic documents are in Lansing, Michigan, at the Historical Commission Archives under *People of the State of Michigan, Ex. Rel. Andrew B. Dougherty, Attorney General vs. The Israelite House of David, a Voluntary Association, et al.,* 5167 (Circuit Court of Berrien County, 1927).

4 Carlisle, "Benton Harbor Remembers."

5 Adkin, *Brother Benjamin,* 321.

6 Mike Martindale. "Feud Over Fortune Embroils Michigan Religious Group," *The Detroit News,* March 6, 2018, https://amp.detroitnews.com/amp/32683303..

7   The author and a coauthor made trips to the campus before and after the renovation. From interviews with Benton Harbor citizens, it appears that the surviving few members of both branches would likely be welcome members in most communities. The historic site sign, placed in front of the second campus (not the stunningly remodeled one) reads: "Mary's City of David: After the death of Benjamin Purnell in 1927, the Israelite House of David religious community split over spiritual direction and accumulation of assets. Purnell's wife, Mary, left and founded Mary's City of David on this adjacent site in 1930. She retained control of four large farms and a ninety-room hotel next to Benton Harbor's expansive fruit market, which provided income for the colony. Between 1930 and 1950, members designed and constructed this complex [now in serious ill repair] of vernacular buildings. At a time when resorts were restricted by race and ethnicity, the colony welcomed Jewish visitors by building cabins and a synagogue to accommodate them and opening vegetarian restaurants that attracted Orthodox Jewish vacationers from Chicago."

8   *Benjamin's Last Writing*, published by the Israelite House of David as reorganized by Mary Purnell, (Benton Harbor, MI: City of David, 1927), 11.

9   *Benjamin's Last Writing*, 9–10.

10 H. M. Williams, *Mysteries, Errors and Injustice at Mary and Benjamin's Israelite House of David,* 1907, 5.

11 Williams, 5.

12 Williams, 5.

13 Adkin, *Brother Benjamin.*

CHAPTER 2

1   Irenaeus, *Against Heresies,* ca. AD 180.

2   Isidore, Origines, 8.5.5; in Stephen A. Barney, *The Etymologies of Isidore of Seville* (Cambridge: Cambridge University Press, 2005), 175.

3   Epiphanius, *Panarion,* 26.6.1.1-2; in Frank Williams, trans., *The Panarion of Epiphanius of Salamis: Book I (Sects 1–46)*, vol. 63, Nag Hammadi & Manichaen Studies (Leiden: Boston: Brill), 90.

4   See also Irenaeus's (d. AD 202) key works, *Against the Gnostics.* Later Clement of Alexandria (d. AD 215) and Tertullian (d. ca. AD 240) attacked the Gnostics as heretics. This collection of works helps us to understand more fully the Gnostics, one of these earliest heresies, and the particular Gnostic sect, the Phibionites.

5   *Pistis Sophia,* 147 and *Second Book of Jeu,* 43.

6   Epiphanius, 26.6.1.1–2, in Williams, 92–93.

7   Epiphanius, (26.6.4.4), 93.

8   Epiphanius, (26.6.4, 5–7), 94.

9   Epiphanius, (26.6.4, 9–5, 1), 94.

10 Epiphanius, (26.6.5.4–5), 95.

CHAPTER 3

1   Paul Megna, "Good Friday Essay: Passion Plays and the Ethics of Spectacular Violence," *The Conversation,* April 13, 2017, http://theconversation.com/good-friday-essay-passion-plays-and-the-ethics-of-spectacular-violence-75916.

2   Martti Nissinen, Robert Kriech Ritner, and Choon-Leong Seow, *Prophets and Prophecy in the Ancient Near East* (Atlanta: Society of Biblical Literature, 2003), 183–185.

3   Daniel Caner, "The Practice and Prohibition of Self–Castration in Early Christianity," *Vigiliae Christianae* 51, no. 4 (November 1997): 396–415.

4   Henry Percival, trans., "First Council of Nicæa (A.D. 325)," Canon 1, from *Nicene and Post-Nicene Fathers* Second Series, vol. 14, edited by Philip Schaff and Henry Wace (Buffalo, NY: Christian

Literature Publishing Co., 1900), revised and edited for New Advent (website) by Kevin Knight, http://www.newadvent.org/fathers/3801.htm.

5 Marvin W Meyer, *The Ancient Mysteries: A Sourcebook of Sacred Texts* (Philadelphia: University of Pennsylvania Press, 1999), 139.

6 John McGuckin, *Westminster Handbook to Origen* (Louisville: Westminster John Knox Press, 2004), 6.

7 Brian Hunt, "A Comparative Pictorial Study of the Wards and Techniques of the Late 13th Century Sword & Buckler Manuscript I.33, or Tower Fechtbuch," The Association for the Renaissance Martial Arts, http://www.thearma.org/Manuals/I33-guards.html#.W14CKNhJGEI.

8 London, British Library MS. Egerton 881 f. 132.

9 Theodoret, *The Ecclesiastical History of Theodoret,* "Concerning the Cunning of Leontius, Bishop of Antioch, and the Boldness of Flavianus and Diodorus," http://biblehub.com/library/theodoret/the_ecclesiastical_history_of_theodoret/chapter_xix_concerning_the_cunning_of.htm. See especially footnote 567.

10 Jane Tibbetts Schulenburg, *Forgetful of Their Sex: Female Sanctity and Society Ca. 500–1100* (Chicago: Univierity of Chicago Press, 2001), 146–147.

11 Mark D. Griffiths, "Religious Self-Harm: A Brief Overview," *Psychology Today* May 4, 2017, https://www.psychologytoday.com/us/blog/in-excess/201705/religious-self-harm.

12 Opus Dei, "12. How Is Penance and Mortification Practiced in Opus Dei?" Interview with Fr. Michael Barrett, May 31, 2006, https://opusdei.org/en-us/video/12-how-is-penance-and-mortification-practiced-in-o/.

13 *BBC News Magazine,* "Why do some Catholics self-flagellate?" November 24, 2009, http://news.bbc.co.uk/1/hi/magazine/8375174.stm.

14 *BBC News Magazine.*

15 Epistle 9.

CHAPTER 4

1 Juju Chang and Spencer Wilking, "Pentecostal Pastors Argue 'Snake Handling' Is Their Religious Right," ABC News, November 21, 2013, https://abcnews.go.com/US/pentecostal-pastors-argue-snake-handling-religious/story?id=20971576.

2 Spencer Wilking and Lauren Effron, "Snake-Handling Pentecostal Pastor Dies from Snake Bite," ABC News, February 17, 2014, https://abcnews.go.com/US/snake-handling-pentecostal-pastor-dies-snake-bite/story?id=22551754.

3 Elizabeth Dias, "Snake Salvation: One Way to Pray in Appalachia," *Time,* September 9, 2013, http://swampland.time.com/2013/09/09/snake-salvation-one-way-to-pray-in-appalachia/.

4 Dias.

5 Chang and Wilking, "Pentecostal Pastors Argue."

6 Julia Duin, "Serpent-handling pastor profiled earlier in Washington Post dies from rattlesnake bite," *Washington Post,* May 29, 2012, https://www.washingtonpost.com/lifestyle/style/serpent-handling-pastor-profiled-earlier-in-washington-post-dies-from-rattlesnake-bite/2012/05/29/gJQAJef5zU_story.html?noredirect=on&utm_term=.f8325bc445c5.

7 Julia Duin, "In W.VA., snake handling is still considered a sign of faith," *Washington Post,* November 10, 2011, https://www.washingtonpost.com/lifestyle/magazine/in-wva-snake-handling-is-still-considered-a-sign-of-faith/2011/10/18/gIQAmiqL9M_story.html?noredirect=on&utm_term=.b3073abdabee.

8 *The Simpsons,* episode 436 "Eeny Teeny Maya Moe," aired April 5, 2009.

9 Andreas J. Köstenberger and Michael J Kruger, *The Heresy of Orthodoxy How Contemporary Culture's Fascination with Diversity Has Reshaped Our Understanding of Early Christianity,* (Peabody, MA: Hendrickson Publishers, 1998); Noel B. Reynolds, "Review of Andreas J. Köstenberger and Michael

J. Kruger, *The Heresy of Orthodoxy: How Contemporary Culture's Fascination with Diversity Has Reshaped Our Understanding of Early Christianity,*" *BYU Studies Quarterly* 51, no. 3 (2012).

10 Bruce Metzger, *A Textual Commentary on the Greek New Testament* (Stuttgart: German Bible Society, 1971), 122–126; Matthew R. Crawford, "Ammonius of Alexandria, Eusebius of Caesarea and the Origins of Gospels Scholarship," *New Testament Studies* 61, no. 1 (January, 2015): 1–29.

11 James Snapp, Jr., "Josh Buice and the Ending of Mark," *The Text of the Gospels,* February 7, 2018, http://www.thetextofthegospels.com/2018/02/josh-buice-and-ending-of-mark.html.

12 Julia Duin, "Christian Serpent-Handlers Protect Us All," *Washington Post,* July 12, 2018, https://www.wsj.com/articles/christian-serpent-handlers-protect-us-all-1531436487.

13 Duin.

CHAPTER 5

1 Zena Simmons, "Detroit's Flamboyant Prophet Jones," *The Detroit News,* September 12, 1997, http://blogs.detroitnews.com/history/1997/09/12/detroits-flamboyant-prophet-jones/.

2 Ibid.

3 Richard Bak, "The Rise and Fall of Detroit's Prophet Jones," *Hour Detroit,* December 6, 2016, http://www.hourdetroit.com/Hour-Detroit/December-2016/The-Messiah-in-Mink/.

4 *Life,* "Prophet's Mink," March 30, 1953, 64–69, https://books.google.com/books?id=CUIEAAAA MBAJ&pg=PA65&dq=prophet+james+f.+jones&hl=en&sa=X&ei=NaiqT4-QM6rI2AX6hdCmAg &ved=0CEkQ6AEwAg#v=onepage&q&f=false.

5 Bak, "Detroit's Prophet Jones."

6 Kevin Mumford, *Not Straight, Not White: Black Gay Men from the March on Washington to the AIDS Crisis,* (Chapel Hill: University of North Carolina Press, 2016), 46–48.

7 Bak, "Detroit's Prophet Jones."

8 Matthew Pehl, "Discovering Working-Class Religion in a 1950's Auto Plant," *The Pew and the Picket Line: Christianity and the American Working Class,* edited by Christopher D. Cantwell, Heath W. Carter, and Janine Giordano Drake (Champaign: University of Illinois Press, 2016), 109–110; The Detroit Industrial Mission (1956–1978) was an ecumenical group that worked to utilize Christian principles in improving labor-owner relations.

CHAPTER 6

1 Michael Doyle, *The Ministers' War: John W. Mears, the Oneida Community, and the Crusade for Public Morality* (Syracuse: Syracuse University Press, 2018), 28.

2 Russell Chandler, *Doomsday: The End of the World—A View through Time* (Ann Arbor, MI: Servant, 1993), 73.

3 Sylvester Bliss, *Memoirs of William Miller* (Laurinburg, NC: St. Andrews University Press, 2005), viii, http://universitypress.andrews.edu/content/Memoirs%20Excerpt.pdf.

4 Bliss, ix.

5 Whitny Braun, "William Miller: The Other Farmer from Upstate New York Who Spawned a Major Religious Movement," *HuffPost,* updated December 6, 2017, https://www.huffingtonpost .com/whitny-braun/william-miller-the-other-_b_9502298.html.

6 Hal Lindsey, "Are We the Final Generation?" *The Hal Lindsey Report,* July 25, 2009, https://www .hallindsey.com/ww-7-25-2009/.

7 Albert Mohler, "False Prophets, False Teachers, and Real Trouble: The Case of Harold Camping," *Albert Mohler* Blog, June 1, 2011, https://albertmohler.com/2011/06/01/false-prophets-false -teachers-and-real-trouble-the-case-of-harold-camping/.

8 Mohler.

CHAPTER 7

1   Robert L. Wise, "Reformation's Apocalypticism: Münster's Monster," *Christian History*, https://
    christianhistoryinstitute.org/magazine/article/reformation-apocalypticism-mnsters-monster. The
    issue is entitled "The End. A History of the Second Coming" and contains seventeen articles that
    may be of interest to those wishing further magazine features on related topics.

2   Wise.

3   Karl Kautsky, "The Anabaptists," chap. 5, part 9 "The New Jerusalem," in *Communism in Central
    Europe in the Time of the Reformation,* (1923; repr. CreateSpace Independent Publishing Platform,
    2017), https://www.marxists.org/archive/kautsky/1897/europe/ch05d.htm.

4   Jeff Starck, "Two Silver Coins in July 1 Auction Recall Bloody End for Supporters of Münster
    Rebellion of 1534," *Coin World,* June 22, 2014, https://www.coinworld.com/news/world-coins
    /2014/06/Two-coins-recall-gruesome-end-to-bloody-Munster-Rebellion-of-1534.all.html.

5   John Howard Yoder, "Zwingli, Ulrich (1484–1531)," *Global Anabaptist Mennonite Encyclopedia
    Online,* last modified September 3, 2013, http://gameo.org/index.php?title=Zwingli,_Ulrich
    _(1484-1531)&oldid=101063.

6   Nanne van der Zijpp, "Beukelszoon, Jan (ca. 1509–1536)," *Global Anabaptist Mennonite
    Encyclopedia Online,* last modified July 31, 2018, http://gameo.org/index.php?title=Beukelszoon,
    Jan(ca._1509–1536)&oldid=144825.

7   Kautsky, *Communism in Central Europe.*

8   Kautsky.

CHAPTER 8

1   Kaufmann Kohler and Samuel Krauss, "Ophites," *Jewish Encyclopedia,* http://www
    .jewishencyclopedia.com/articles/11720-ophites.

2   Gedaliahu A. G. Stroumsa, *Another Seed: Studies in Gnostic Mythology,* Nag Hammadi Studies 24,
    (Leiden: Brill, 1997), 6, 10. https://books.google.com/books?id=9ZU3AAAAIAAJ&pg=PA5&lpg
    =PA5&dq=ophitism&source=bl&ots=UKpGAlX4ag&sig=y_K7LkCPiUpvDxrN8UJoEMcSW58
    &hl=en&sa=X&ved=0ahUKEwjVqOSN3LLbAhXLtVMKHUIDA6AQ6AEIZjAI#v=onepage
    &q=ophitism&f=false. Their redrafting of the biblical texts is akin to the fantastic (bizarre) story of
    the Mesopotamian Enkidu and Tiamat.

3   Irenaeus, *Against Heresies*, I:4.3–7.

4   Irenaeus, *Against Herecies, III*, Preface.

5   Bettany Hughes, *Helen of Troy: The Story Behind the Most Beautiful Woman in the World* (New York:
    Knopf Doubleday Publishing Group, 2005), 15, https://books.google.com/books?id=K8PCYtg1So
    cC&pg=PT501&lpg=PT501&dq=Ennoia+and+helen&source=bl&ots=CKarb0Cr7Y&sig
    =vX_OdwJJgo1_zi2eAM2NCorMi5w&hl=en&sa=X&ved=0ahUKEwiv1uLgoancAhXF54MKHZ
    L1CkAQ6AEIbjAP#v=onepage&q=Ennoia%20and%20helen&f=false.

6   Sinope, modern Sinop, is located on the northern edge of modern Turkey's side of the Black Sea.
    Marcion's influence in churches, and much of his personal involvement, took place in Asia Minor
    that is much of modern-day Turkey. This area was also part of the ancient area of Anatolia.

7   Carpocrates lived in Alexandria, Egypt, during the first half of the second century AD.

8   As the studies of ancient religious texts have shown, established scholars sometimes have lively
    and often unsettled debates over a text's authenticity—and the *Secret Gospel of Mark* is among the
    most controversial. Peter Steinfels discusses three books on this question in his *New York Times*
    article, "Was It a Hoax? Debate on a 'Secret Mark' Gospel Resumes." The "resumes" refers to three
    recent publications whose titles give their theses: *The Gospel Hoax: Morton Smith's Invention of
    Secret Mark* (Waco, TX: Baylor University Press, 2005) and *The Secret Gospel of Mark Unveiled:*

Imagined Rituals of Sex, Death, and Madness in a Biblical Forgery (New Haven, CT: Yale University Press, 2007) challenge its authenticity, while another vehemently defends it: *Mark's Other Gospel* (Waterloo, Canada: Wilfrid Laurier University Press, 2005).

9   Peter J. Williams, "An Introduction to Mark's Gospel," Theology Network, 2008, https://www
.theologynetwork.org/biblical-studies/starting-out/an-introduction-to-marks-gospel.htm.

10 Larry Jimenez, "10 Bizarre Early Christian Sects," Listverse, February 7, 2014, https://listverse
.com/2014/02/07/10-bizarre-early-christian-sects/.

11 Edwin M. Yamauchi, professor emeritus of history at Miami University (OH), is one of the key voices in modern history on the interface of Gnosticism and Christianity. In his evaluation of the sources, contrary to the work of Elaine Pagels and others, he demonstrates Gnostic threads as heretical offshoots of first-century Christianity, not underpinning or influencing its formation. See *Pre-Christian Gnosticism: A Survey of the Proposed Evidences* (1973; repr., Eugene, OR: Wipf and Stock, 2003). See also the works of Simon Gathercole, fellow of Fitzwilliam College, Cambridge (reader in New Testament studies and directory of theological studies), such as *The Gospel of Thomas: Introduction and Commentary* (Leiden: Brill, 2014) and *The Gospel of Judas* (Oxford: Oxford University Press, 2007).

12 John Wesley, "Preface to *Sermons on Several Occasions*," in *John Wesley,* ed. Albert C. Outler, (New York: Oxford University Press, 1964), 89.

CHAPTER 9

1   R. I. Moore, *The Birth of Popular Heresy,* (Toronto: University of Toronto Press, 1995), 28, https://
books.google.com/books?id=zz1MbStmeZkC&pg=PA28&lpg=PA28&dq=tanchelm+heresy&sour
ce=bl&ots=D9ARMkC11g&sig=OqABUQ66OULrHJr5ItP9iRgHW_M&hl=en&sa=X&ved
=0ahUKEwivo9_Z57fbAhVSZKwKHQjMANgQ6AEIUDAH#v=onepage&q=tanchelm
%20heresy&f=false.

2   For more in-depth studies of medieval manuscripts and documents, scholars have access to the wonderful repository at Saint Louis University, the Knights of Columbus Vatican Film Library (more than thirty thousand manuscripts on microfilm), plus the bonanza of filmed images of Jesuit historical documents.

3   There are various theories about the fertile social and the economic and religious dynamics of medieval society for apocalyptic or radical biblical interpretations. A general introduction to medieval culture and events brings these more into perspective but does not nullify the heresy of various views. See C. Warren Hollister, *Medieval Europe: A Short History,* 7th ed.(New York: McGraw-Hill, 1994), and for a wide-ranging look and lively read filled with anecdotes, see Susan Wise Bauer, *The History of the Medieval World: From the Conversion of Constantine to the First Crusade* (New York: W. W. Norton and Company, 2010).

4   Moore, *The Birth of Popular Heresy,* 30.

5   Moore, *The Birth of Popular Heresy,* 30. See also Austin P. Evans and Walter L. Wakefield, trans. and eds., *Heresies of the High Middle Ages: Selected Sources Translated and Annotated* (New York: Columbia University Press, 1969), 96–100.

6   Moore, "Tanchelm: Letter of the Canons of Utrecht, 1112-14," in *The Birth of Popular Heresy,* 29.

7   Moore, 31.

8   A helpful introduction to the veneration of saints is Peter Brown, *The Cult of the Saints: Its Rise and Function in Latin Christianity,* Haskell Lectures on History of Religions (Chicago: University of Chicago Press, 1981); the multifaceted role of saints in the Middle Ages mirrored in many respects the patronage system of the late Roman period.

9   St. Norbert is also the progenitor of the highly ranked Catholic institution in Wisconsin—
St. Norbert College, https://www.snc.edu/.

10 Moore, "Tanchelm," in *The Birth of Popular Heresy*, 31.

11 Moore, *The Birth of Popular Heresy*, 31.

12 Adriaan Bredero, *Christendom and Christianity in the Middle Ages* 3rd ed., trans. Reinder Bruinsma (Grand Rapids, MI: William B. Eerdmans, 1994), 3.

13 A wealth of resources articulate this development. The Medieval Institute at Notre Dame, with around eighty faculty members from the university participating, produces a trove of recourse annually around its mission, "research and teaching on the multiple cultures, languages, and religions of the medieval period." Its robust medieval studies library collection and Conway Lectures provide a regular stream of research and scholarship on the complex nature of the societies (and religious communities) in which heretical and often bizarre cult leaders arose. Its Medieval Institute Library has over one hundred thousand volumes and nearly all its partner library's collection in digital format—The Ambrosian Library in Milan, Italy. Another prominent center is the Medieval Institute at Western Michigan University, host of the massive annual International Congress on Medieval Studies. Its "About" page notes, "The Medieval Institute at Western Michigan University ranks among the top ten of the some 90 institutes, centers, and programs focusing on medieval studies in North America." Its Medieval Institute Publications provide a space for exploring "what it has meant to be human through the ages."

14 Bredero, *Christendom and Christianity in the Middle Ages*, 4.

15 Richard Landes, "The Birth of Heresy: A Millennial Phenomenon," *Journal of Religious History* 24, no. 1 (February 2000): 26–43.

16 Landes, 341–342.

17 For an accessible volume capturing ten key voices, see Michael W. Holmes, *The Apostolic Fathers in English*, 3rd ed. (Grand Rapids, MI: Baker Academic, 2006). For more general primary sources, see C. Warren Hollister, Joe Leedom, Marc Meyer, and David Spear, *Medieval Europe: A Short Sourcebook*, 4th ed. (New York: McGraw-Hill, 2001).

18 Kenneth Schenck, *Understanding the Book of Hebrews: The Story behind the Sermon*, (Louisville, KY: Westminster John Knox Press, 2003).

CHAPTER 10

1 Alma White, *Klansmen: Guardians of Liberty* (Zarephath, NJ: Pillar of Fire Church, 1926), 160.

2 Alma White, *Heroes of the Fiery Cross* (Zarephath, NJ: Pillar of Fire Church, 1928), 121.

3 Ryan Hamlett, "The Graham Stephenson House," HistoricIndianapolis.com, September 24, 2013, http://historicindianapolis.com/the-graham-stephenson-house/.

4 "Our Story," ABOUT US page, Englewood Christian Church, http://www.englewoodcc.com/history.html.

5 White, *Heroes of the Fiery Cross*, introductory material.

6 White.

7 My wife and I restored the last remaining house associated with the historic black community in the nearby town of Weaver, Indiana, a community featured in various African American history discussions. Although the WikiMarion editors and article author call it the "Pattengale House," it is actually the "Bowman Farm," based on its founding. See: http://wikimarion.org/Pattengale_House. Weaver ceased to exist officially in 1929, the year before America's last public lynching took place seven miles north in downtown Marion, Indiana. In 1923, the Imperial Wizard of the KKK (national leader), Hiram Wesley Evans, inducted David C. Stephenson as Grand Dragon of Indiana. This took place at a massive ceremony just twenty miles due west of the Weaver farm, in Kokomo, Indiana on July 4 (one hundred thousand in attendance). During Weaver's heyday, with around four thousand inhabitants, one of its three churches was Wesleyan.

8 White, 9.

9   White, 14.

10 White, 18.

11 White, 73.

12 White, 137.

13 White, 136–137.

14 White, 138.

15 White, 138.

16 White, 142.

17 White, 143.

18 White, 29.

19 White, 68.

20 White, 72.

21 White, 72.

22 Douglas O. Linder, "The 'Mississippi Burning' Trial: An Account," Famous Trials, http://www
    .famous-trials.com/mississippi-burningtrial/1955-home.

23 Linder.

24 Alma White, *The Ku Klux Klan in Prophecy* (Zarephath, NJ: Pillar of Fire International, 1925),
    45–48.

25 White, *Heroes of the Fiery Cross*, 156.

26 White, 4.

27 White, 106.

CHAPTER 11

1   Less than a century earlier, the Muslims of Aleppo slaughtered the Crusaders from Antioch
    in the infamous Battle of the Field of Blood in which the Muslims of Aleppo slaughtered the
    Crusaders from Antioch (1119). Roger of Salerno, the regent ruler of Antioch, died at the foot of
    his standard, the great jeweled cross, after taking a sword to his face. All but two of his nearly five
    thousand men were captured or killed.

2   Thomas F. Madden, "The Venetian Version of the Fourth Crusade: Memory and the Conquest of
    Constantinople in Medieval Venice," *Speculum* 87, no. 2 (April 2012): 312.

3   Niketas Choniates, *O City of Byzantium, Annals of Niketas Choniates*, trans. H. J. Magoulias"
    Choniates, trans. H. J. Magoulias (Detroit: Wayne State University Press, 1984), 316–317. For a
    helpful collection of sources online, and introductory narratives, see https://lsa.umich.edu/content
    /dam/cmenas-assets/cmenas-documents/K-14-Educational-Resources/Crusades%20Secondary
    %20Ed%20Lesson.pdf.

4   David L. Riggs, email interview on Latin terminology, June 11, 2018.

5   Encyclopedia of Britannica Editors and Grace Young, "The Siege of Zara," *Encyclopedia Britannica*,
    https://www.britannica.com/event/Siege-of-Zara.

6   Choniates, *City of Byzantium*, 316–317.

7   Robert de Clari, ch. lxxiii–xxiii, in Carl Hopf, *Chroniques Gréco-Romanes* (Berlin: Weidmann,
    1873), 57–58, https://sourcebooks.fordham.edu/source/4cde.asp.

8   Choniates, *City of Byzantium*, 15–16.

9   Kate Connolly, "Pope Says Sorry for Crusaders' Rampage in 1204," *The Telegraph,* June 30, 2004,
    https://www.telegraph.co.uk/news/worldnews/europe/italy/1465857/Pope-says-sorry-for-crusaders
    -rampage-in-1204.html.

10 Pope Innocent III, ep 136, Patrologia Latina 215, 669–702, trans. James Brundage, *The Crusades:
    A Documentary History* (Milwaukee, WI: Marquette University Press, 1962), 208–09; cited in
    The Medieval Sourcebook, Fordham University, https://sourcebooks.fordham.edu/source
    /1204innocent.asp.

NOTES

11 W. H. C. Frend, *The Rise of Christianity* (Philadelphia: Fortress Press, 1984), 324.

12 Jerry Pattengale, "Indulgence," in Pattengale, J. Bradley Garner, and Lisa Velthouse, *Straight Talk: Clear Answers about Today's Christianity,* 2nd ed. (Marion, IN: Triangle Press, 2008), 224.

13 Pattengale, Garner, and Velthouse, 224–225. It is important to follow the modern dialogue between the major branches of Christianity, and not relegate doctrinal understanding (differences) to these medieval decisions alone. In *Straight Talk,* the authors summarize this: "Official dialogue between Catholics and Protestants about the meaning of salvation has been taking place in recent years. By identifying overreactions in both branches of Christianity and by genuinely seeking common ground, bridges of understanding are now being built. For an evangelical Catholic's perspective, you might consult Keith Fournier's 'Evangelical Catholic: A Contradiction in Terms?' (in *Evangelical Catholics,* 11–23). In May 1999, the Catholics signed the Catholic-Lutheran Accord, which represents a major step in resolving the difference between Protestants and Catholics on how one is made righteous in the sight of God," 34.

14 Byron H. DeMent and Edgar W. Smith, "Repent" *ISBE.* 4: 136.

15 Roland H. Bainton, *Here I Stand: A Life of Martin Luther* (New York: Mentor Books, 1950), 54.

16 Nathan W. Bingham, "Justification by Faith Alone: Martin Luther and Romans 1:17," Ligonier Ministries, https://www.ligonier.org/blog/justification-faith-alone-martin-luther-and-romans-117/.

17 Sarah Pulliam Bailey, "Campus Crusade Changes Name to Cru," *Christianity Today,* July 19, 2011, https://www.christianitytoday.com/ct/2011/julyweb-only/campus-crusade-name-change.html.

CHAPTER 12

1 As a long-time judge of the Evangelical Christian Publishers' Christian Book Award, I was pleased to see the following book among the 2017 finalists. Printed by the Bible Society Australia. It provides perhaps the best glimpse of hope for the Christian ministries and partnerships in the continent today—a stark cry from the episodes highlighted in this chapter. I encourage all readers to consult this book (a work of art itself) and other resources from the Bible Society Australia to see the vibrancy of Christianity today among the people of Australia: Louise Sherman and Christobel Mattingley, eds., *Our Mob, God's Story: Aboriginal and Torres Strait Islander Artists Share Their Faith* (Sydney: Bible Society Australia, 2017); "For over 50,000 years Aboriginal & Torres Strait Islander people across this great land we now call Australia, have been celebrating in their stories, sons and ceremonies. . . . In this book 66 artists from over 40 First Nations of Australia share their vision of Christ, human and divine," 17.

2 James Bonwick, *The Last of the Tasmanians* (London: Sampson Low, Son and Marston, 1870), 400; John Harris uses the stronger word while citing this—"haunt us today" in John C. Harris, *One Blood: 200 Years of Aboriginal Encounter with Christianity—A Story of Hope* (Claremont, CA: Albatross Books, 1990), 86. This book is invaluable in the study of the Aborigines.

3 William Ridley, *Kámilarói and other Australian Languages* (Sydney: Thomas Richards, 1875), 171.

4 Thomas Dove, "Moral and Social Characteristics of the Aborigines of Tasmania," *Tasmanian Journal of National Science* 1, no. 4 (1842): 249, cited in John Harris, "Justice, Aboriginal Land Rights, and the Use and Abuse of Scripture," *The Occasional Bulletin of Nungalinya College, Darwin,* no. 38 (1987): 9, originally published in *Zadok Perspectives,* (1987).

5 Dove, cited in Harris, *One Blood,* 24.

6 Dove, cited in Harris, *One Blood,* 25.

7 Harris, *One Blood,* 89.

8 We could discuss various places worldwide where these horrible events happened. Eminent historian Justo L. Gonzalez writes: "It was one of the bleakest times in the history of Christianity. In the name of Christ, thousands were slaughtered, millions enslaved, entire civilizations wiped out. When the first Europeans settled in Hispaniola, there were some 100,000 native inhabitants on the island. Half a century later, there were scarcely 500. In Mexico, in seventy-five years the

population declined from more than 23 million to 1.4 million; in Peru, in fifty years, from 9 million to 1.3 million." Justo Gonzales, "Lights in the Darkness," *Christian History*, 1992, https://www.christianitytoday.com/history/issues/issue-35/lights-in-darkness.html.

9   Tanya Riches, "Redeeming Australia Day: How Aboriginal Christians are Challenging Australian Spiritually," ABC Religion and Ethics, January 25, 2016, http://www.abc.net.au/religion/articles/2016/01/25/4394002.htm.

10 Harris, "Justice," (1987), 8. The final quote is taken from Dove, "Aborigines of Tasmania," 249.

11 Riches, "Redeeming Australia Day."

12 Riches.

13 Harris, *One Blood*, 24.

14 Anti-Hypocrite, *Sydney Herald*, October 5, 1838, quoted in Harris, *One Blood*, 27.

15 Juror, *Australian,* December 8, 1838, quoted in Harris, *One Blood*, 27.

16 "Death of King Boongarie," *Sydney Gazette,* November 27, 1830, National Library of Australia, https://trove.nla.gov.au/newspaper/article/2196620.

17 "Death of King Boongaire."

18 Harris, *One Blood*, 54.

19 Harris, 55.

20 J. E. Stanton, "Mt. Margaret: Missionaries and the Aftermath," in T. Swain and D. Rose, eds., *Aboriginal Australians and Christian Missions* (1988): 292–307 (see 303), cited in Harris, *One Blood*, 849.

21 Harris, *One Blood*, 852.

22 The Bible's translation for the Aborigines and nearly all people groups is perhaps best displayed in the "Illuminations" room at the Museum of the Bible in Washington, DC (opened November 2017). The various translations are displayed both digitally and in print through a creative color-coded system.

23 E. S. Parker, *The Aborigines of Australia* (Melbourne: Hugh McColl, 1854), cited in Harris, *One Blood*, 175–176.

24 Parker, cited in Harris, 176.

25 Sherman and Mattingley, *Our Mob*, 18.

26 Sherman and Mattingley, 18. One of the more telling aspects of this book and the difficult interactions between most of the early missionaries and the Aborigines is represented on page 115, in the discussion of Ellen Draper's painting, "Healing." The editors' explanation notes that "Ellen depicts the healing power of Jesus bringing hope and new life to his Aboriginal people. There is no Scripture translated in Ellen's heart language of Kamilaroi but in 1856 William Ridley [whom we met earlier] translated a story about Jesus into Kamilaroi. . . . (Note that Ridley replaced Jesus with Immanuel because Jesus was unpronounceable to Kamilaroi speakers)," 114.

27 Harris, "Justice," 9–10.

28 Bartolomé de Las Casas, *In Defense of the Indians: The Defense of the Most Reverend Lord, Don Fray Bartolomé de las Casas, of the Order of Preachers, Late Bishop of Chiapa, Against the Persecutors and Slanderers of the Peoples of the New World Discovered Across the Seas*, trans. and ed. Stafford Poole (DeKalb: Northern Illinois University Press, 1974), 176.

ABOUT THE AUTHOR

JERRY PATTENGALE: MA, Wheaton College; MA & PhD, Miami University (OH); History—Ancient Near East (mentor—Edwin Yamauchi). Jerry is author or editor of over 30 books, has produced numerous videos and international projects, and has contributed to various leading venues like *Washington Post, Wall Street Journal, History Channel, Christianity Today, RNS, Chicago Tribune,* and *InsideHigherEd.* He serves as the executive director of education for the Museum of the Bible (one of its two founding scholars), and Indiana Wesleyan University's first University Professor. The Azusa Pacific University student body twice named him "Faculty Member of the Year," in addition to "Honors Society Professor of the Year." The National Resource Center (USC) selected him for its National Student Advocate Award, the National Endowment for the Humanities for its research award to Isthmia, Greece, and he received AP and Hoosier State Press Association awards for his twenty-year news column. He was a pioneer nationally for pur-pose-guided education (*Why I Teach* and *Purpose-Guided Student,* McGraw-Hill, *Visible Solutions for Invisible Students,* USC, *Helping Sophomores Succeed,* Jossey-Bass, etc.). He serves on the boards of Religion News Service and the Jonathan Edwards Center (Yale), is long-time associate publisher for *Christian Scholar's Review,* and the executive director of NationalConversations.com and the Lumen Research Institute. He also holds distinguished appointments at the Sagamore Institute, The Moody Center (Northfield, MA), Gordon-Conwell Theological Seminary, Excelsia College (Australia), and Tyndale House, Cambridge. His books in 2017–2018 (authored, co-authored, or editor) include *Faith Made Real* (WPH); *Global Impact*

Bible (Worthy); *The World's Greatest Book: How the Bible Came to Be* (Worthy); *The Book: The Narrative, History and Impact of the Bible* (4 vols., Museum of the Bible, DC); *The Bible in Augmented Reality* (2 vols., Compedia, Ramat Gan, Israel); *The Bible and Its Impact on Western Culture* (2 vols., Museum of the Bible, DC); *Telling the Truth with a Smile: Volume 4—Life Happens* (DustJacket), the 2018 theme issue for *CSR*; and *The State of the Evangelical Mind* (IVP). Forthcoming with Johnnie Moore (and John Foxe) is *The New Book of Christian Martyrs* (Tyndale House). He graduated from high school at 16 and homeless, a story featured in the PBS/WIPB special, *Leading the Way out of Poverty*. His mantra in his purpose-guided work reflects this journey, "The dream needs to be stronger than the struggle."

ABOUT THE COAUTHORS

NICHOLAS DE NEFF received his Master of Arts degree from Andover Newton Theological School. He served as an independent writer, researcher, and contributor to the *Global Impact Bible* (Worthy Publishing), *BibleJourney* (NC), *The Bible in Augmented Reality* (2 vols., Compedia, Ramat Gan, Israel); and *The Book: The Narrative, History and Impact of the Bible* (4 vols., Museum of the Bible, DC).

DANIEL FREEMYER obtained his Master of Divinity from Duke Divinity School and received his Ph.D. from Fuller Theological Seminary in Old Testament and Ancient Near Eastern Hermeneutics. He is the author of *Prophetic Messages by Festivals: Rhetorical Ideologies in Prophetic Texts* (Fuller Dissertation Series; CATS 2018) and contributor to *BibleJourney* (NC). Daniel currently serves as adjunct professor of Biblical Interpretation at Wesley Seminary at Indiana Wesleyan University.

IF YOU ENJOYED THIS BOOK, WILL YOU CONSIDER SHARING THE MESSAGE WITH OTHERS?

Mention the book in a blog post or through Facebook, Twitter, Pinterest, or upload a picture through Instagram.

Recommend this book to those in your small group, book club, workplace, and classes.

Head over to facebook.com/WorthyPublishing, "LIKE" the page, and post a comment as to what you enjoyed the most.

Tweet "I recommend reading #IsTheBibleAtFault by @Jerry Pattengale // @worthypub"

Pick up a copy for someone you know who would be challenged and encouraged by this message.

Write a book review online.

WORTHY®
PUBLISHING

Visit us at worthypublishing.com

twitter.com/worthypub

worthypub.tumblr.com

facebook.com/worthypublishing

pinterest.com/worthypub

instagram.com/worthypub

youtube.com/worthypublishing